SMASHED UP AND BURNT DOWN BARS.

THE RAILWAY HOTEL, WEALDSTONE.

THE STORY OF AN ICONIC PUB AND MUSIC VENUE

By

LAYNE PATTERSON

Copyright Layne Patterson

Layne Patterson has asserted his right under the Copyright, Design and patents Act 1988 to be identified as the author of this work.

All rights reserved. No part of this publication may be reproduced, stored in a retrieval system or transmitted, in any form or by any means, without the author's prior permission in writing.

This book is sold subject to the condition that it shall not, by way of trade or otherwise, be lent, resold, hired out or otherwise circulated without the authors prior consent in any form of binding or cover than that in which it is published and without a similar condition, including this condition, being imposed on the subsequent purchaser.

Every reasonable effort has been made to trace copyright holders of material reproduced in this book, but if any have been inadvertently overlooked the author would be glad to hear from them.

layne.patterson64@g.mail.com

also by the author:

QUADROPHENIA – The Complete Guide

QUADROPHENIA (at 40) – The Complete Guide

INDEX

1. *INTRODUCTION AND IDENTITY CRISIS.*
2. *FOREWARD BY 'IRISH JACK'.*
3. *WEALDSTONE – A POTTED HISTORY.*
4. *THE RISE AND DEMISE OF THE RAILWAY.*
5. *THE MUSICAL LEGACY OF THE RAILWAY.*
6. *THE WHO/HIGH NUMBERS.*
7. *REMEMBERING THE RAILWAY.*

INTRODUCTION AND IDENTITY CRISIS!

As a massive fan of The Who it's always pleasing to know that a massive part of their early history can be directly linked to your home-town. However, it's not quite so pleasing when the venue that people refer to is claimed to be in Harrow and Wealdstone!

For the record, and for people who need to be informed (obviously not you dear reader) there is no such place as Harrow and Wealdstone, yes there is a train station bearing that particular moniker, but no actual place exists of that name! Wealdstone is simply a district within the borough of Harrow, so Harrow and Wealdstone station is therefore in Wealdstone, which is in Harrow. Easy isn't it?

As a lifelong fan of Wealdstone Football Club (The Railway Hotel was also important in their early history) the thought of having the word Harrow anywhere near our title would be sacrilege! I believe there is another club somewhere in South Harrow that call themselves Harrow Borough (a title they are more than welcome to – although title is not a commonly used word in them there parts), however, on to the towns oldest and biggest club. Wealdstone fans are used to being called Wealdstun , Willsstun etc, etc (a fact that would have been further complicated if a planned relocation to nearby Willesden some years ago happened) so if you learn nothing else from this book please note that The Railway Hotel was in Wealdstone – and please also pronounce the last part as STONE! – Many Thanks!

Any historical references to The Railway Hotel being in Harrow and Wealdstone, will, however remain as this was how it was reported by some at the time.

The Railway Hotel stood proudly like a beautiful big white cathedral perched on the highest point in Wealdstone, right on top of the bridge, and looked down at all that she surveyed. It was a place that was to play a massive part in the very history of Wealdstone! I would certainly never have classed myself as a regular of the Pub, early drinking days were at The Royal Oak and then Wealdstone Social Club (both now sadly gone!), but I can say that I spent many late nights in its basement club, known at the time as The Sidings. It was this place that many would descend to once the Pubs were shut to round of things until the early hours! I must have seen dozens of bands play there over the years, and do you know something I can't remember any of them! There was one particular band that would play there in the early to mid-eighties who were pretty damn good, but sadly I never knew their name! The Sidings had long since lost its reputation as a top music venue and was now simply a place for a late night drink. A massively popular venue with the local Irish community – a good night could be virtually guaranteed!

Talking of the Irish community, there is one man who springs immediately to mind, built like the proverbial 'brick outhouse' he would always great you with a handshake that almost broke every bone in your hand – he was the legendary, Jimmy Kane. I recall once seeing him coming out of the nearby Mario's café to board his dumper truck full of sand and slabs, it had been parked on the kerb like you would do with a car, the usual 'hand-break' welcome was extended, and he told me he was off to lay a patio for somebody in Harrow Weald. A few minutes later I passed by the Railway Hotel and noticed the same dumper truck half on the road half on the path. It seems the temptation to pass the Railway without a quick pint was just too much for old Jimmy. Several hours (at least 6!) later as I was walking past the Pub I noticed the vehicle still unmoved, and heard the unmistakable roar of his riotous laughter emanating from inside! Apparently, Jimmy and the building materials were still there well into the early hours of the next morning, and possibly somebody in Harrow Weald is still waiting for a new patio! RIP Jimmy, a tough but fair man, who always made me smile.

How many people were aware of the important part this place had played in the history of British music, and what a key role it had in the worst peace-time rail disaster in history? The answer was probably not many, in the upstairs bar there once hung a framed cover of Meaty, Beaty, Big and Bouncy, the LP by The Who that immortalised the Railway Hotel. Apart from this token gesture many people would have been totally oblivious to the credentials of this famous old boozer!

On a Sunday in February 2000, I was on my way back from my son's football match when I saw the plumes of smoke on that fateful afternoon as the long closed building ended its days in the saddest way possible! I remember thinking - what a big part of our history had gone forever!

Birthdays, Weddings and even Wakes, I saw them all there, and was even chucked out of there one night whilst dressed as Batman, in my defence it was actually more likely this was due to the actions of my future brother-in-law, Stan – who was dressed as Noddy!

On my way to Wembley Stadium in the summer of 2019 I drove past the old place on my way to see The Who in a sold-out concert, but oh what I would have given to have seen them at the Railway! The Railway Hotel in Wealdstone will mean many things to many people, for me it's just nice to have spent some time in a place that was an important part of the history of the finest band to have ever graced our turntables! Heartfelt thanks to all who have helped with memories and information, some chose not to be involved (and I fully respect their decision), also apologies if any of the following may inadvertently cause painful memories to return – but EVERYTHING I have included was already in the public domain anyway!

This book is dedicated to everyone who ever spent some time (however short) in this famous and never to be forgotten old pub but in particular:

Liz

Irish Jack (a legend and a gentleman)

John Patterson (you lucky old sod you saw The Who there!)

Graham Sharpe (a former member of my Uncle John's gang and a constant and welcome guiding hand)

Deirdre Maher (my cousin who loved the place, and was invaluable in my research for this book!)

And to the memory of:

Sam (Denis) Patterson – a Wealdstone man all of his life

And

Keith Moon – the finest Keith Moon type drummer to have played at the Railway Hotel

Also

Emily Collyer and Margaret Akam – two remarkable ladies in the Railway Hotel's history

And lastly but not least:-

Stan, John, Caroline, Mick and many others! – Some great times were had in your fine company within them walls!

THE RAILWAY HOTEL MAY BE GONE BUT ITS LEGACY LIKE THE MEMORIES WILL LIVE ON FOREVER!

THE RAILWAY SIDINGS c1994 – MICK RYDER (STEWARD OF THE NEARBY WEALDSTONE SOCIAL CLUB), THE AUTHOR, AND JIMMY? THE FORMER TWO WEARING JUMPERS VERY MUCH OF THEIR TIME!

FOREWARD

IRISH JACK REMEMBERS THE RAILWAY HOTEL

A reading by Irish Jack to the Festival Tours visitors who had travelled from the United States to London to follow folk rock band Fairport Convention's annual English tour. The trip to the Railway Hotel in Harrow and Wealdstone was arranged during a day off and coincided with the 25th anniversary of The Who. This is an extract from Irish Jack's reading to his seated audience in the original basement room where Railway Hotel gigs were held......

In 1964, Richard Barnes, otherwise known as 'Barney' ran this venue as a successful Rhythm and Blues club. Barney had attended Ealing Art College studying graphic design with The Who's lead guitarist Pete Townshend. Together they shared a first floor apartment in Sunnyside Road near the art college. It is Richard Barnes himself who is the sole author of the band name 'The Who'. Previously called The Detours since first forming in 1962 the band saw a Brighton-based band called The Detours on the TV pop show 'Thank Your Lucky Stars' and realised a name-change was inevitable. The band had a meeting to discuss the name change. Original drummer Doug Sandom suggested 'The Chisel -Toe Men' a sly nod to the stylish young men who were wearing the current Cuban-heeled boot - he was out voted. Pete Townshend wanted the band to be called 'Hair' since long hair was a contentious subject among the ranks of the discerning press and anyone over the age of 30. Doug Sandom had a brainwave. "How about 'The TEDS'...the first letter of our surnames?" "Who?" inquired Roger Daltrey who'd been half listening to the latest ramblings! "That's it !" shouted an excited Richard Barnes, "The Who. It's perfect." The others looked at each other unsure as Barnes continued, "Look, it's only three letters. You can use them as big as you want." A couple of nights later as The Detours finished their stint at the Oldfield Tavern in Greenford, Lou Hunt the pub compere who had a penchant for getting as many puns as possible out of a band's name addressed the audience saying.. "Don't forget folks they're back next week and all roads lead to The Detours." Roger poked him in the ribs, "We've changed our name, Lou. We're The Who now." Lou Hunt looked confused. "Who?" "Yeah, The Who," Roger replied. Lou immediately went into top gear..."Ladies and gentlemen, who's up here next week? The crowd shouted back, "The Detours!" "No. I said Who's up here next week?"

When The Who had their Tuesday night residency here in this very room we are sitting in, they began it on the 30 June 1964 billed as 'The Who'. They then changed their name under the auspices of their new manager Peter Meaden and performed here as The High Numbers from 14 July to their last gig here on 22 September 1964. Peter Meaden was a publicist who worked on and off for Andrew Loog Oldham a resident publicist for the Rolling Stones. Meaden who came from Palmers Green in London was one of the early Mods who frequented Mod clubs like the Discotheque, the

Flamingo and the Scene in Ham Yard...all along the Wardour Street strip in London's Soho. He went on to coin the phrase - 'Mod is an aphorism for clean living under difficult circumstances'. Peter Meaden thought up the name The High Numbers and persuaded The Who to adopt the Mod lifestyle (Pete Townshend was already a Mod). A picture of a poster in Richard Barnes' book 'The Who - Maximum R&B' advertises The High Numbers at this venue the Railway Hotel, Harrow and Wealdstone, with admission at three shillings and sixpence. A few weeks later they increased it to four shillings.

If you look up you're looking at the famous ceiling. This is the ceiling in which Pete Townshend had a close encounter with during their residency in 1964. After playing the Railway for a couple of weeks the band were getting fed-up with the temporary stage extension which consisted of beer crates and table tops each time they had to set up. So they paid for a proper stage to be built by a carpenter. These new arrangements gave them a more solid and secure feeling for their increasingly physical stage act and also had a bit more room. However, it was slightly higher than the original stage and the ceiling was always notoriously low. According to Pete Townshend here's what happened : "I started to knock the guitar about a lot, hitting it on the amps to get banging noises and things like that and it started to crack. I banged it against the ceiling and it smashed a hole in the plaster. The guitar neck actually poked a hole through the ceiling plaster. When I brought it out the top of the neck was left behind. I couldn't believe what had happened. There were a couple of people from art school whom I knew at the front and they were laughing their heads off. One of their girlfriend's was staring up at me like 'flash git'. So I just got really angry and got what was left of the guitar and smashed it to smithereens. About a month earlier I'd managed to scrape together enough money for a 12-string Rickenbacker which I'd only used on two or three numbers. It was lying at the side of the stage so I picked it up, plugged it in and gave them a sort of look and carried on playing as if I'd meant to do it.

THE RAILWAY HOTEL PHOTOGRAPHED BY IRISH JACK IN 1988

One Tuesday night in mid-September Barnes was surprised to see a posh well-dressed gentleman standing at the admission table. He was looking around him as though he wasn't sure where he was. Barnes sensed he might be from the local council inspecting the premises. If he was, Barnes was in trouble. To add atmosphere to the basement room Barnes had it hot, sweaty and dark. The only lights were from two orange coloured bulbs and the radiators were turned up full with windows blacked out. It was a pilled-up Mod's paradise. The stranger with the Oxbridge accent inquired. "Is it always like this?" Barnes became worried unsure of what to say. He was already aware he had broken several safety laws for crowded venues. The guy was reaching into his pocket.....a notebook perhaps to issue a summons? Instead he drew out a very expensive silver cigarette case and offered a jaw-dropped Richard Barnes a cigarette. "I'm Kit Lambert. What's the name of the band?" Later Barnes and Peter Meaden followed Lambert out into the courtyard. He explained that he and his business partner Chris Stamp (brother of actor Terence Stamp) were on the lookout for a suitable band to film as part of a documentary. Barnes and Meaden were very impressed. Lambert stood at the edge of the floor watching the Mod boys and girls dancing and slowly an idea began to blaze in his head. He stayed for twenty minutes, left and got into his red Mini Cooper. His partner Chris Stamp was in Dublin filming 'Young Cassidy'. That night Kit Lambert phoned him excitedly. In a few days it was the weekend. Stamp caught a Saturday flight back to London and together they managed to catch the last fifteen minutes of The High Numbers at the Watford Trade Union Hall!

IRISH JACK.

IRISH JACK AND PETE TOWNSHED c 1971

I am truly indebted to 'Irish' Jack Lyons for this unique and great memory of The Who's time at the Railway Hotel. Anybody who has even a vague interest in The Who will know exactly who Irish Jack is, but for the uninitiated Jack is probably the group's most famous fan! A devoted disciple who was there at the very first gigs, and soon became a friend of its members, in particular Pete Townshend! It is thought that the song entitled 'Happy Jack' is their homage to him and it is also believed that the character of Jimmy in Quadrophenia is heavily based on him. Many thanks Jack –LP.

A POTTED HISTORY OF WEALDSTONE

Mention Wealdstone nowadays and most people will probably think of its famous Football Club of the same name, and its forever linked own home-grown celebrity - The Wealdstone Raider! Wealdstone Football Club were formed in 1899, playing at various venues in its home town before residing at Lower Mead Stadium for some seventy years – thereafter a nomadic existence eventually saw them safely ensconced at a new home in nearby Ruislip.

The Club that took its name from its birth place has had many ups and downs during its lifetime including a glorious season in the mid-eighties when they became the first club to clinch the non-league double. At time of writing this famous old club are back in the top echelons of non-league football plying their trade in the National League. England Legend Stuart Pearce and footballer turned actor, Vinny Jones are amongst its many famous old-boys.

THE HISTORY MAKING WEALDSTONE F.C. TEAM IN 1985

Everything that Wealdstone, was to become can be directly traced to the birth of the Railway system in the area. Indeed, another not quite so welcome claim to fame is that it can also sadly boast the worst peace-time rail disaster, which in 1952 claimed some 112 lives!

Two hundred years ago the area that would later become Wealdstone was little more than a rural district a couple of miles to the north of Harrow on the Hill, the later, at the time for all intents and purposes was Harrow's Town Centre. Some years later the nearby lower slopes of Greenhill would earn that particular title!

The mid 1830's was to see the London-Birmingham Railway expanding at an increasingly rapid rate, but there was a desperate need to have more stops enroute between the two major cities, with Harrow identified as the perfect first stop from the capital! However, with the hill far from ideal for laying railway tracks the pastured and flat area that would later become Wealdstone was deemed to be perfect! Incidentally, it would be a further 47 years, in 1880 before Harrow Town Centre had its own railway, when the Metropolitan line eventually arrived and was somewhat misleadingly named Harrow-on-the-Hill, with locals very soon christening it as Harrow-Met.

Wealdstone, as we know it today, was the land nestled between the two parishes of Harrow Weald and Harrow. The boundaries of the two adjoining parishes being marked by a sarsen stone known as the Weald Stone, the stone still remains in that exact spot to this day. A Weald is in fact another name for a wooded area, with this particular one being commonly known as Weald Stone. The Weald Stone is actually estimated to be around ten thousand years old, and is not thought to be native of this area, with theories that it was relocated from somewhere to the west of England, where they were much more prevalent. The Weald Stone is located outside a former pub called The Red Lion, later on renamed The Weald Stone Inn. A popular Curry Restaurant now inhabits the premises, which incidentally, is just a few yards away from the birth place of a certain Ian Dury!

THE ANCIENT SARSEN STONE THAT WOULD EVENTUALLY GIVE WEALDSTONE ITS NAME

With the proposed location of Harrow Weald station identified, plans were very quickly submitted for what would eventually become the gateway to the new industrialised area of Harrow. With its new found easy access Wealdstone very soon saw major companies relocating or opening in the area. Her Majesty's Stationery Office (HMSO), Kodak, Whitfriars Glassworks, Hamilton's Brush Factory as well as, Windsor and Newton Brushes were major employers in the now thriving Wealdstone, with Kodak going on to employ in excess of six thousand people in its fifties heydays!

The Victorian High Street became a bustling place with six pubs all within easy walking distance of the station, sadly none of which remain today!

The Iowa was the first to go sometime in the sixties, which was followed by The Duke of Edinburgh the following decade. The Queens Arms (just across the road from the aforementioned, and a few yards from the Station) was so popular with commuters back in the day that its bar staff would pull off Ale into large buckets and ladle it into glasses to save time. The Queens Arms, which later on its life was called Sam Maguire eventually felt the decline in its business to such an extent that it was also forced to close for good and demolished a couple of years ago. Currently its land is awaiting the inevitable flats to be built.

A GREAT OLD PHOTO OF WEALDSTONE HIGH STREET SHOWING ITS THREE LONG LOST PUBS

Further along the High street was The Case is Altered, smack bang next door to the former Police Station and Magistrates Court. The Case is Altered had a few gestations as various other bars and restaurants before being closed for good, with the site now being the home of the local Poundland. Peel Road, just off the High Street was the home of The Royal Oak, which has traded as an Indian restaurant for a number of years now. The Daddy of all of Wealdstone's drinking establishment was, of course, The Railway Hotel (more of which later!), there have been various bars open (and close !) along the High Street over the years, including one named the Sarsen Stone, which was a member of the J.D. Wetherspoons company, the bar still remains but is now in different ownership. Barretts is the oldest (and in many people's opinion the best) of the 'new' bars to have emerged! An Irish bar, many ex-patrons of The Railway were to relocate there following its demise. Barretts further embodies the spirit of The Railway with its signage calling it 'Railway Bar'.

BARRETTS BAR – STILL FLYING THE FLAG FOR THE RAILWAY

Various shops and business outlets have come and gone in the High Street over the years such as Fine Fare, Presto and Woolworths to name but a few. In 1962 the site of a furniture shop on the corner of Grant Road and the High Street was immortalised in a film entitled, Live Now Pay Later, which starred Ian Hendry and Liz Frazer. The building used remains to this day, and is now a convenience store.

It's possible that this film may even have been shown at one of Wealdstone's three cinemas that it boasted back in the day! The Odeon was towards the north of the High Street before it closed in 1961, and was eventually demolished to make way for an Office block. The Herga was slightly nearer the High Street having been built at the start of the Second World War and closed just twelve years later. The building still remains, and is now a retail outlet for electrical products and instantly recognisable! The old Dominion (or to some ABC) is right on the edge of Wealdstone before it becomes Harrow, some years ago when the Multiplex was opened in Harrow it was closed and reopened as an Indian cinema. This last bastion of Wealdstone's cinematic history was covered in a lurid blue cladding in the early sixties hiding its beautiful art-deco frontage. However, a redevelopment of the site including keeping part of the cinema has been mooted with plans to remove the cladding and restoring it to its former glory!

THE DOMINION CINEMA BACK TO ITS FORMER GLORY IN THE NEAR FUTURE - HOPEFULLY!

The station which also had original plans to its north for its own Hotel was actually opened as just Harrow in 1838. The station very soon became known as The Weald by locals and ultimately soon changed its name to Harrow and Wealdstone in recognition of its fast growing surroundings! Wealdstone in its current location came into being around 1870, by which time a small Village had grown to in excess of 200 houses!

Harrow and Wealdstone station has the dubious honour of being the location of the worst peacetime rail crash which occurred on 8th October 1952, and claimed 112 lives with a further 340 injured!

A train collision involving three trains during the morning rush hour at precisely 8.19am was to cause carnage with the impact so great it forced the station clock to stop dead on that time! The overnight express train from Perth crashed at high speed into the rear of a local passenger train standing at a platform forcing the ensuing wreckage to block the adjacent lines, very soon after the wreckage was hit by an express train travelling north at 60 mph.

It later transpired that the Perth train had passed a caution signal and a further two danger signals before the impact occurred. The many fatalities were taken to an emergency requisitioned mortuary at the adjacent Railway Hotel (more details of which appear later on in this book) with emergency services flooding the area from amongst other places the nearby US air force base in Ruislip. After many years of campaigning a memorial was finally unveiled to commemorate the lives lost that fateful day in 1952.

THE MEMORIAL PLAQUE OUTSIDE HARROW & WEALDSTONE STATION AND THE DEVASTATING CARNAGE THAT HAPPENED ON THAT FATEFUL DAY IN 1952

Up until the late eighties Wealdstone still remained much unchanged with its easily identifiable Victorian buildings right throughout the High Street. Indeed many of the shops still trading were in fact Victorian built houses and just plonked a frontage on onto what was affectively their front garden! Remembrance Sunday was always a big deal at the small clock tower/war memorial in Wealdstone, and I can clearly remember how packed the place would be as a child. The clocktower was built in 1923 as a memorial to local soldiers that lost their lives in the First World War. The clocktower was opened by, and dedicated to local MP, Oswald Mosley. Mosley was to have a chequered political career, which saw him go on to lead the notorious Fascist Party in Britain. The nearby Civic Centre would eventually become the Towns focal point for remembrance Sunday, but somehow it never felt quite the same!

WEALDSTONE CLOCK TOWER AND WAR MEMORIAL COMMEMORATING 248 LOCAL MEN WHO DIED ON ACTIVE SERVICE

During the seventies various redevelopment plans were to be mooted in an area that was clearly in need of some sort of regeneration, and in the 1990's a by-pass was commissioned and built to make Wealdstone a more pedestrian friendly area.

The by-pass certainly had the desired effect, as people started to do just that, and passed by the once bustling Wealdstone High Street in their droves! The disastrous decision to divert people away from Wealdstone ultimately sounded the death knell for Pubs, Shops and various other businesses' alike! Many feel that the decline and trouble hot-spot that Wealdstone descended into can be directly attributed to the decision to by-pass it back in the nineties!

Sadly, in recent years Wealdstone has suffered from continued anti-social behaviour and crime (some of which has been quite major); many unsavoury incidents have even gone onto make national headlines. Big companies such as McDonalds and Wetherspoons simply just had enough and sadly left the area!

Hopefully, sooner rather than later Wealdstone will be re-born again into the thriving and more importantly safe area that its very name was previously synonymous with. Harrow Council, apparently, are said to be keen to address these issues and have begun a lengthy consultation period that may well see Wealdstone returning to somewhere near its former glories!

THE RISE AND DEMISE OF THE RAILWAY

The Harrow Weald station (shortly after its opening known as Harrow station, and eventually to be called Harrow and Wealdstone) opened for business on 20th July 1837, but in a largely undeveloped area was poorly served with local amenities. The nearby Queens Arms very soon prospered with the new footfall in the area, and would serve the eager and thirsty patrons with Ale ladled straight into their glasses from buckets.

In January of the following year, the London & Birmingham railway made it known that they were prepared to lease a portion of its land to any interested party with the view of building a Hotel / Inn to capitalise on the burgeoning trade that the new station was enjoying. The land that was available was in or around what is now the car park area of the station's back entrance, although this was at one time its main entry point. For whatever reason this never materialised, and the Queens Arms would continue to dominate the requirements of the station's thirsty passengers for another good few years!

Subsequently local land owner and farmer Henry Finch Hill made available for sale a prime piece of his estate right on the boundary of railway owned land. Henry Finch Hill was a major landowner and a member of the gentry of Harrow on the Hill, as well as having the esteemed title of Guardian of the Parish. Whether he ever enjoyed a drink in the new establishment on his former land is not known! In 1853 The Railway Hotel was built, and indeed opened the same year. A large sized building was constructed to include rooms; at least three separate bars, an off-licence and a grand function room. An unmade slope was eventually replaced with proper stairs for easier access to the stations entrance, and for a while the front area of the Hotel stood as a solitary building.

Possibly the very first licensee of the Railway Hotel was a Mr T.Comley who was certainly in the post in 1861 when he organised the event below, a grand pigeon shoot with the winner receiving either a cash sum or a whole pig!

> **PIGEON SHOOTING, AT HARROW**
> TO BE SHOT FOR, at Mr. T. Comleys, Railway Hotel, Harrow Station, on Thursday, April 4th, a FINE PIG, value £8. Sixteen members, at 10s. each. The winner to receive £7 10s., or pig. Mr. S. Hammond will supply the birds. A Sweepstakes afterwards at sparrows. On the event of wet weather a large marquee will be erected, and every accommodation for sportsmen and their friends will be provided on the ground.

The following map (c1863) shows the Railway Hotel for the first time, with the surrounding land to its side still in the ownership of Henry Finch Hill.

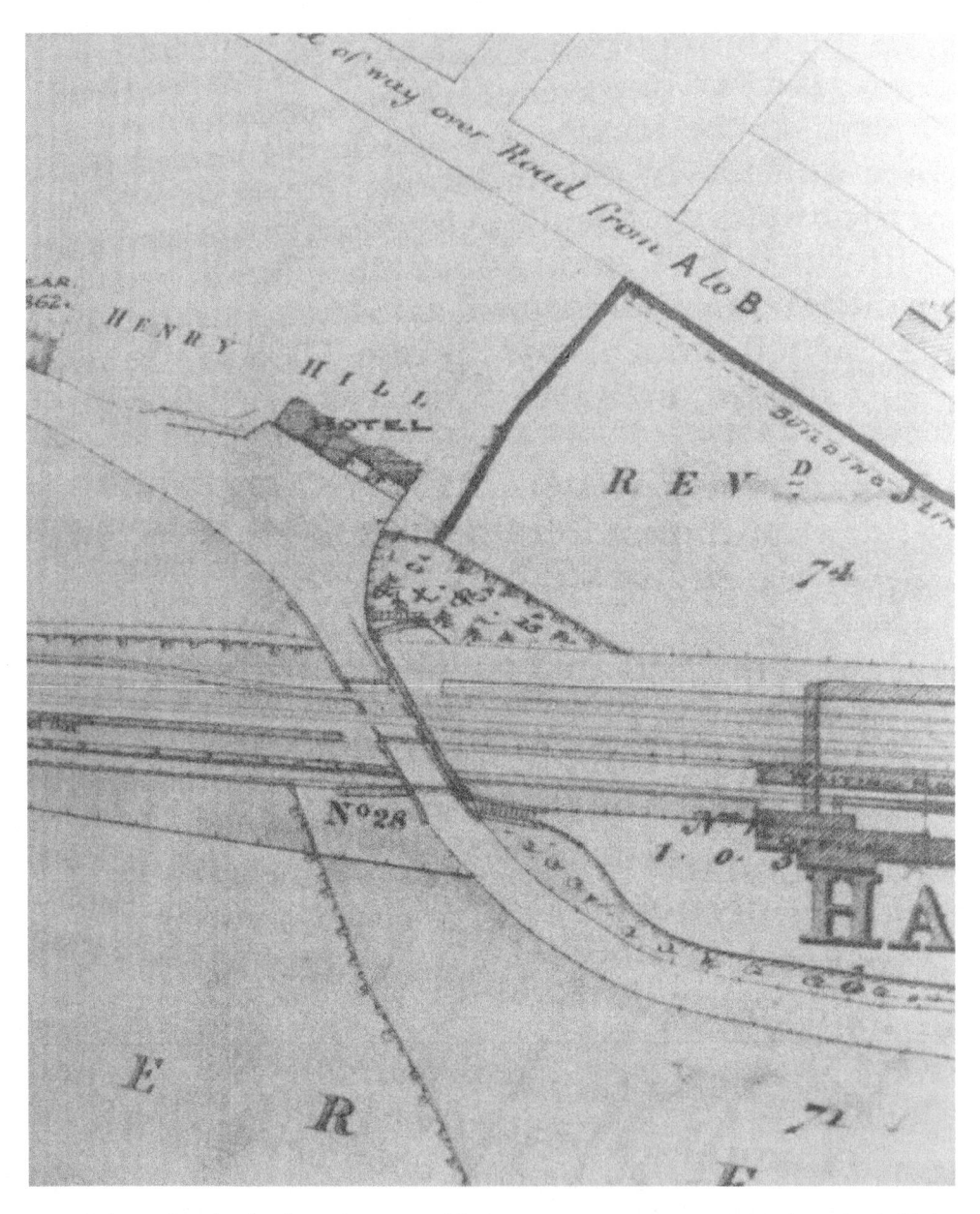

One of the earliest landlords of the new public house was a certain James Marlow who held the licence until 1878 when he was succeeded by James Uridge. In 1880 it is likely that Mr Clarke had just taken over as licensee when he very soon found himself in hot water (no pun intended) with the local Highway and Sanitary department, Clarke had upgraded the drainage and soil pipes at the Railway Hotel, neither of which were deemed to be acceptable, and an order was made to carry out the repairs or risk a hefty fine. This would appear to have been the only recorded incident of his time at the Hotel before he was succeeded four years later by Lewis Cole and his wife Emma who made the short journey from the Malden Hotel in Watford to take over.

In 1884 during Cole's early days as a licensee he was to find himself in Court as a witness following the first recorded incident of fighting at the Railway Hotel. The court report below details an incident when Henry Edward Fountain was charged with assaulting John Hall Roberts. The two men became embroiled in an argument when Fountain stepped in to remonstrate with Roberts who had rebuked his son for the heinous crime of forgetting to wear his hat!

EDGWARE

PETTY SESSIONS – JULY 30TH

(Before C.D.E. Fortnum Esq, (in the chair), T.C.Baring Esq, M.P., and R.Miller Esq, Q.C.)

CHARGE OF ASSAULT.

Henry Edward Fountain, of the Temperance Coffee House, Wealdstone was summoned for assaulting and beating John Hall Roberts on July 19th.

Mr B.E. Greenfield defended.

Complainant stated that he went into the Railway Hotel, Harrow, on the evening of the 19th July. His son came into the house for some ale, and he scolded the boy for coming without a hat. Defendant was standing close by and interfered, when witness told him he was addressing his own son. Defendant then went into the hotel and called for some drink, but they refused to serve him, and also declined to give him a light. He left the house, and witness also went out. He was about to give him a light, when the latter struck him violently to the face. His eyebrow was cut open and also his cheek. He was knocked down, and his thumb was put out, and his knee cut. He went home, and remained in bed for six days in consequence of the assault.

By Mr Greenfield: He was honorary secretary to the Wealdstone Cricket Club. He would not swear that he was drunk or sober on the night in question. It was not a fact that he told defendant to go out; it was absurd to suppose that he was 'chucker out' at the hotel; he did not understand the prisoner. It was not a fact that he fought with a man named Buckingham the previous Saturday, and received two black eyes. He had no conversation with the defendant after the assault. He saw him kick his white hat away, and was only too glad that his own head was not in it.

Lewis Cole, the landlord of the Railway Hotel, said the defendant had previously used bad language in the house. He did so on the evening in question, and witness refused to serve him. He shortly afterwards left the house. Subsequently he heard that Mr. Roberts had been assaulted, and went to the bridge and there saw him bleeding. Witness accompanied him home, and he went to bed, after bathing himself for about half-an-hour.

Annie Robinson, an assistant in the bar at the hotel, said she refused to serve defendant. He came back later on, and spoke of having assaulted Mr. Roberts. Mr. Greenfield stated that the complainant was drunk, but that defendant was sober. Complainant pushed him out of the bar, and some words passed, but they parted on friendly terms. Mr. Roberts staggered against something, and fell down, saying 'Oh dear! Oh dear!' He, however, got up and walked home. Witness would swear that the defendant did not assault him

At the conclusion of the case, the magistrates fined the defendant 40s. With 26s. 61. Costs.

The following month on 15th August disaster nearly struck at the Railway Hotel when it suffered its first recorded fire. A coal fire in one of the rooms had got out of hand and was discovered just in time before any real damage was done!

In or around 1891 the railway Hotel changed hand again with J.H. Hodgson taking on the role of landlord. Little is known about his time in charge which lasted until 1892, save for a brief visit to court in 1891 when he was awarded £3.10s in damages against a local drover (type of shepherd), Thomas Beecham who took offence to being pelted with water every time he entered the premises. Beecham finally snapped at this constant provocation and smashed the main bar window as an act of revenge. Towards the end of 1892 Hodgson left to take over another Railway Hotel in nearby Sudbury, the licence being transferred from a George Hodgson, possibly his father.

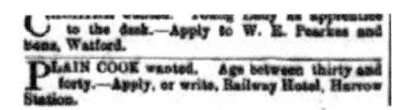

AN ADVERT IN 1892 LOOKING FOR A PARTICULARLY SPECIFIC TYPE OF COOK

In 1892 Mr George Lander took over as licensee and within three years had secured the freehold of the property from Mr Ernest Owers for £3130 with a ground rent of £120 per annum over a forty nine year lease. Four years into his tenure George Lander took out the following advertisement to boost trade, and as you can see (in the following advertisement) Horses were also well looked after! Very soon after taking over George Lander applied for a music licence which had been recently refused, the Railway Hotel had previously held one for over seven years, but had for some reason let it lapse. After a successful reapplication music was once again permitted.

"RAILWAY HOTEL,"
WEALDSTONE.

Adjoining Harrow Station L. & N. W. Rly.

LARGE COFFEE and DINING ROOMS

Luncheons, Dinners, Teas, Chops and Steaks provided on the shortest notice.

Good Stabling.   Lock up Coach-house.

AGENT FOR

Benskins Celebrated Watford Ales.

Proprietor - GEORGE LANDER.

THE ABOVE ADVERT WAS INCLUDED IN THE HARROW OBSERVER MARCH 1896

However it would appear that George Lander only remained in full control for around three years before Mr Weight took over the Freehold of the land, with George Lander possibly remaining as licensee before eventually moving onto another unknown Pub in the Willesden area. Within a year George Lander was on the move again to The White Lion Hotel in Waddesdon near Aylesbury in Buckinghamshire. The lease was then briefly transferred to C.T. (Thomas) Andrews in 1898, who alongside his wife remained as landlords for little more than a year before moving onto the George Inn in Enfield. Thomas Andrews was yet another landlord to end up in court as the following report from a hearing at Brentford County Court in 1903 (some years after the event) details:-

THE WELCOME GUEST.
AMUSING COUNTY COURT CASE.

At the Brentford County Court, on Friday, before His Honour Judge Shortt, K.C., Chas. Thomas Andrews, of the "George Inn," Enfield Town, sued Edwin Woodbridge, a tailor, of 148, Ecclestone-road, Ealing, for £5 12s., money lent and goods sold. There was a counter claim for work done. The plaintiff was represented by Mr. C. Hathaway, and Mr. C. Almond was for the defendant.

Mr. C. Hathaway said that in 1898, the plaintiff was the landlord of the Railway Hotel, Harrow, and the defendant used that house for the purposes of his business as a tailor. The parties were on friendly terms, and in 1898 plaintiff advanced £3.10s. to the defendant. The following Christmas the defendant ordered a case of whisky.

Plaintiff bore out his solicitor's statement, and cross-examined by Mr. Almond, admitted having two suits of clothes from the defendant, but they, together with the items charged for in the counter claim, were paid for by the cheque for £6 5s. (produced).

Defendant said that some years ago he was in the habit of staying at the Railway Hotel, Harrow for weeks together. At that time he had plenty of money, and when he left the house, Mr. Andrews used to write to him, asking him to come back, as trade was so bad, and he (Andrews) could not fill the smoking room. On one occasion, when he had spent all his money, and only had sufficient to take him home, and was about to leave the house, Mrs. Andrews took his hat off his head and said "You don't leave this house to-night," and added, "If it is money you want, you can have it." Next morning she advanced him £3 10s. and he stayed on for some time. With regard to the claim for whisky, the plaintiff was desirous of selling his house, and told him that if he could get £1,000 for it he would make him a present of £100. Meanwhile, as he had been such a good customer to him, he would send him a case of whisky. This present never arrived, and two days after Christmas witness sent a telegram, asking if it was coming. Next day the case arrived. The cheque (produced) was given to witness by the plaintiff in settlement of the account of a man named Payne. To support this statement, defendant produced a note-book, containing orders on behalf of Payne, in the plaintiff's writing.

Cross-examined by Mr. Hathaway, defendant stated that he was never charged for his board and residence at the Railway Hotel, as the plaintiff was only too glad to have him there.

Plaintiff denied that the cheque, which was one of his own, represented money, handed to him for defendant by Payne. Defendant was always charged for his board and residence.

His Honour examined the note-book produced by the defendant, and looking at the entry with regard to Payne's order inquired, "What does four fresh men mean?"—Defendant: I really don't know. Perhaps Mr. Andrews does. It is in his writing.

Mr. Andrews denied all knowledge of the matter.

His Honour held that plaintiff was entitled to succeed with regard to his claim of £3 10s., as it was admitted to have been received from Mrs. Andrews. With regard to the case of whisky, it was not unlikely, considering the friendly terms the parties had been on, that it was a present from the plaintiff to the defendant, and, therefore, that would not be allowed. As to the counter claim, he would adjourn that to the next court, in order that Mr. Payne might be called.

The early history of the railway hotel saw it being used for a variety of other activities including both a Law and Coroners court. The nearby Railway station had seen its fair share of tragic accidents (with the inquiries invariably held at the Railway Hotel) such as the one involving a Jockey by the name of George Tilley. Tilley had attempted to alight a moving steam train and misjudged the distance falling to his death between platform and train. In 1870 there was a further accident at the nearby Station resulting in seven deaths, the inquest again being held at the Railway Hotel. Surely, though, one of the saddest inquiries heard at the Railway Hotel Coroners Court was that of the suicide of a 22 year old man by the name of Henry Hill in 1895. The following report from the St James Gazette is very much of its time, with his suicide being blamed on temporary insanity having previously been subject to a stay in a 'lunatic asylum'.

THE HARROW TRAGEDY.
INQUEST AND VERDICT.

At the Railway Hotel, Harrow, yesterday, Dr. Gordon Hogg, the West Middlesex coroner, opened an inquest on the body of Henry Hill, aged twenty-two, described as a shorthand-writer, lately residing at 178, Vauxhall Bridge road, who committed suicide by throwing himself in front of a London and North-Western train at Kenton Bridge, between Wembley and Harrow stations, on Friday last.

The first witness was Harriet Hill, of Woburn Sands, Bucks, who identified the body as that of her son, whose full name was Henry Thomas Hill. He had been lately following the occupation of a journalist. The deceased had suffered for some years from the effect of over-study and had at one time to become a patient at the Prestwich Lunatic Asylum, near Manchester. The witness had, however, never heard of his having threatened to commit suicide, although he had been very much depressed and was given to avoiding people's society. The witness knew nothing of the circumstances of her son's death, except what she had read in the newspapers.

At this stage the young lady, Miss Smith, who was engaged to the deceased, entered the court, and was about to take her seat in the witness-box when the sound of the whistle of a passing train was heard, and, throwing up her arms with a scream, she swooned. She was removed in a hysterical condition to a bed-room of the Railway Hotel.

Daniel Carter, a platelayer, said that he found the body of the deceased after the train had passed. He saw a young lady (Miss Alice Smith) on the bridge, and, on asking her who it was, she replied, "It is my Harry; where is he? can I see him?" The witness said "No," whereupon she replied, "I must see him," and ran to the other side of the bridge and tried to climb over the fence. The witness prevented her doing this, and held her till some other men came and removed the mutilated body from the rails.

Ann Edwards, of 283, Vauxhall-bridge-road, said that Miss Smith took lodgings at her house over a week ago, and she was in the habit of going out in the morning and not returning until night. A day or two after her arrival she was sobbing bitterly, and the witness asked her what was the matter. She replied that she had come to London to get married, and had paid for a special licence, but added, "Now he won't have me till I am over my trouble." A day or two afterwards she went out and met Hill, and on returning remarked cheerfully, "He has thought better of it, and is going to give notice for us to be married at a registry office to-morrow." On the Friday she left home at a quarter past ten A.M. to meet her lover at Mount-street, Grosvenor-square. Since the tragedy the young lady had informed the witness that when they arrived at the registry office Hill would not go in, but took her for a long walk in the country. He had all her money, and she said she would not leave him till she got it back. Speaking of what occurred at Harrow, she told the witness that when they got on the Kenton bridge she asked Hill for her money. He threw it at her, saying, "Now I'll leave you:" and then jumped over the fence. That was the last she saw of him.

Ernest Perris, of the London News Agency, said that the deceased had been in his service up till July. He received a salary and witness had always found him conscientious and hard-working. The witness did not know he was in want of money. The deceased had written one or two stories of a melancholy and morbid character, amongst them being "A Young Man's Struggle for Life," and "A Life for a Life."

The jury returned a verdict of Suicide whilst temporarily insane.

THE COLLYER ERA

In 1899 the Hotel changed hands yet again with H.F. (Henry) Collyer taking over the mantle. It is likely that the pub was a freehouse during this period as not only could you drink the local fare from Benskins brewery, but also those on offer from Watney Coombe and Reid. The Collyer family would prove to be a significant part of the Railway Hotel's history remaining there for some eighteen years.

There may well have been a few people over the years to have had their collars felt by the local constabulary for driving a car after taking a drink from the Railway Hotel, but maybe not that many for driving a horse and cart. The following report from the local press details an incident whereby Mr Collyer had asked the police to eject a local man after which he attempted to make his way home with said form of transport. A hefty fine was the reward for not walking the short distance home! It would seem that there were a good few visits to the courthouse during Henry Collyer's time at the helm, but he worked hard to retain the reputation of the Railway Hotel and became a much respected publican amongst his peers.

> **TOO DRUNK TO DRIVE.**
>
> Arthur Bateman, 29, of 22, Stirling-road, Wealdstone, a carman, was charged with having been drunk while having the care of a horse and cart on the 27th ult.—P.C. Windsor, 706 X, said he was called to eject the prisoner from the Railway Hotel, Harrow. Having got him outside, witness found prisoner had charge of a horse and cart and accordingly took him into custody. Prisoner was obstreperous, and during a slight struggle witness received a blow on the eye, not of a very severe character.—The Magistrates took a lenient view of the assault, and fined prisoner 10s. and 3s. 6d. costs for being drunk.

With people starting to enjoy more organised sporting activities Mr Collyer attempted to woo various local institutions, including Wealdstone Football Club, (mentioned in detail later) the following advertisement was also taken in the local press in 1906 to try and entice local Athletic Clubs. Four years later a bowls club was even started, playing briefly in land to the rear of the Hotel.

> **To ATHLETIC CLUBS.** — Try the Railway Hotel, adjoining Harrow (L. and N.W. Railway) station, for a summer's outing. Central, commodious and convenient. Large garden for use of private parties only, not accessible to the public. Luncheons, teas and dinners by arrangement. Write proprietor.

The name of H.F.Collyer is evident in the centre of the following picture taken in or around 1906. At the turn of the new century the area to the left of the picture began to develop with the newly opened Wealdstone Social Club and Institute, and a small cluster of shops, so now The Railway was effectively part of a small shopping parade. The area was known as Station Approach.

AN EARLY IMAGE OF THE RAILWAY HOTEL c 1906 STILL WITH ITS ORIGINAL FAÇADE – THE LADY IN THE CENTRE IS POSSIBLY EMILY COLLYER

To the left of the picture you will see the Order Office; these were forerunners to Off Licences, and had a separate entrance to the main pub when it opened in 1906. The following advertisement heralds this new venture in the local press of November 1906. In 1908 with the Order Office and Railway Hotel flourishing, benefiting greatly from the ancillary trade from its neighbouring business's, and as part of general works by the council to improve the bridge area, a tarred footpath was laid outside the entrance for the very first time. The Wealdstone Bridge shopping area had now grown into a very busy little entity!

There were of course still the regular visits to the local courtroom including one involving a well-known man in and around Wealdstone, Frank Attenborough. Attenborough had been barred from virtually every local hostelry but would still attempt to enter them and use bad language when he was ejected. A further attempt to enter the Railway Hotel saw him once again ejected and the police called. In court he was described as 'one of a class of men who were a nuisance to the district' a hefty £5 was levied with the option of taking a 4 weeks prison sentence with hard labour instead!

The Railway Hotel,
WEALDSTONE.

A NEW ORDER OFFICE

For Bottled Beers, Wines and Spirits.

NOW OPEN!!

Premises adjoining the Hotel, with a Separate Entrance for customers, have been fitted up with every convenience to meet the demands of the neighbourhood.

Single Bottles of all Wines & Spirits.
AND
Watney Combe, Reid & Co.'s
CELEBRATED ALES & STOUTS
supplied.

H. F. COLLYER,
Wine & Spirit Merchant.

WANTED, a Boy to make himself generally useful in house and garden; sleep out.— Apply, Railway Hotel, Wealdstone.

AN ADVERT FROM THE HARROW OBSERVER FOR STAFF IN EARLY 1907

On the 8th December 1908 Henry Collyer attended a pre-Christmas Dinner for local publicans and was now regarded as a man with fine business acumen. The Railway Hotel was now a thriving business and the envy of many! Sadly just seven days later he died suddenly in his room at the Railway Hotel at the tragically young age of 54. Henry's widow, Emily must have had a terrible time with the festive season just about to start, but was lucky to have been able to take on a Manager by the name of Thomas Silvester who ensured that the business, at least, remained intact!

Emily Collyer was obviously a woman of substance and shared her late husband's business skills as she dusted herself down, and pushed the flourishing Hotel to even greater heights. Musical concerts and dances were now a regular feature at the Railway Hotel and Emily even branched out into external catering, another great success!

CONCERT AND DANCE

AT

The Railway Hotel, Wealdstone,

NEXT SATURDAY EVENING.

MR. CHARLES BOLTON announces his second Concert and Dance on the Lawn in the rear of the Hotel.

UP-TO-DATE SONGS BY EXCELLENT COMPANIES.

ADMISSION 3d.   -   -   GARDEN ENTRANCE.

AN ADVERT FOR A CONCERT AND DANCE FROM 1909

Emily Collyer had made such a success of the Railway Hotel that she decided to purchase another similar business, the Chorleywood Hotel, and continued to run both hostelries in tandem even during the First World War which started in July, 1914. Emily was known to be a fair woman to work for and even when her trust was misguided (as below) she refused to press charges against an employee who decided to see the New Year in with a pretty hefty nightcap!

LOCAL PETTY SESSIONS.

TUESDAY, JANUARY 4, 1916.

Before Messrs. C. W. Matthews (in the chair), G. Sneath, G. Acton Davis, T. Charles, J. S. Hogg, J. Walter Smith, J. H. Searcy and Sir William Crump.

THEFT BY A BARMAID.

Alice Henderson, Railway Hotel, Wealdstone, was charged with stealing half a bottle of whiskey and half a bottle of gin, value 4s., the property of Mrs. Collyer.

Mrs. Collyer said the prisoner had been in her employ as a barmaid. On January 1 she went to the prisoner's bedroom and found an empty half bottle of whiskey and the prisoner in bed drunk. Under her pillow she found half a bottle of gin. She did not wish to press the charge.

Detective-sergeant Owen said the prisoner admitted taking the gin.

Prisoner, who said she was very sorry and would sign the pledge, was bound over to be of good behaviour for twelve months.

REPORT FROM THE HARROW OBSERVER JANUARY 7th 1916

In October 1917 with the end of the War still over a year away Emily Collyer decided to sell the Railway Hotel to Henry Hulks. Emily had a massive part in making the Railway Hotel a much sought after business and decided to sell up and concentrate fully on the Hotel in Chorleywood. However, as you will read in the following report (note – the dates are inaccurate!) it was only a short time before she was to pass away following complications of an operation. Emily Collyer's contribution to the history of the Railway Hotel cannot be underestimated in any way, bearing in mind she never lived long enough to exercise her right to vote in a general election, she was indeed a strong woman with supreme business skills in a very much male dominated environment.

> DEATH OF MRS. COLLYER.—It is with great regret that the news will be received that Mrs. Collyer, late of the Railway Hotel, has passed away, at her hotel at Chorley Wood. Mrs. Collyer with her late husband, Mr. H. F. Collyer, came to Wealdstone about thirteen years ago when they purchased the Railway Hotel. For many years it was conducted by them, and the death Mr. H. F. Collyer occurred somewhat suddenly about four years ago. Mrs. Collyer, who was a woman of singular business ability, then purchased Chorley Wood Hotel and the two houses were very ably conducted by her. A few weeks ago she sold the Railway Hotel and was intending to devote her time to assisting with the house at Chorley Wood. Unfortunately she became seriously ill and an operation was found necessary. She was taken to hospital where the operation was successfully performed, but soon after returning home she passed away greatly regretted and respected by all who knew her. The funeral took place on Tuesday at Nunhead in the presence of many sympathising friends. Messrs. J. A. Massey and Son carried out the funeral arrangements.

THE DEATH OF EMILY COLLYER AS REPORTED IN THE HARROW OBSERVER NOVEMBER 9TH 1917 – A POWERFUL LADY IN THE HISTORY OF THE RAILWAY HOTEL

There were also many other things that the Railway Hotel was employed for, including its use for local council meetings, various sports clubs and local institutions also made use of its facilities. The Railway Hotel was also used regularly as an auction house with sales of both livestock and butchered products. Local companies would also hold sales for various materials with tree wood and timber a particularly popular event. There were also regular land auctions held at the Railway Hotel with many parts of the rapidly developing neighbourhood being sold there.

The following sales notice relates to land that was just over the bridge towards Harrow, facing what was later to become the Civic Centre.

Freehold Building Land,
HARROW, MIDDLESEX.

MESSRS. RODWELL & SON

Have received instructions to Sell by Auction, at the Railway Hotel, Harrow Station, on Monday, the 11th June, 1888, at 6 for 7 o'clock in the evening, in one lot, a valuable plot of

FREEHOLD BUILDING LAND, close to the London and North-Western Station, having a frontage of about 78 ft. to the main road, and a depth of about 100 ft., known as lots 3, 4, 5, and 6, of the Ferndale estate, and is the only portion of that estate available for the erection of business premises, for which there is so much demand in this neighbourhood.

May be viewed at any time prior to sale. Particulars and conditions of sale may be had at the Railway Hotel, Harrow Station; at the usual Inns; of T. J. Broad, Esq., solicitor, Watford; and (free by post) of the Auctioneers, 164, High-street, Watford, Herts.

Like most pubs at the time the Railway Hotel was able to enjoy pretty relaxed trading times, with many opening all day. However, in 1872, the Intoxicating Liquor (Licensing) Bill was introduced which reduced pub licensing hours dramatically, all day drinking was now a thing of the past! The Government were seemingly worried that some employees were choosing to have extended meal breaks and often returned in no fit state to operate machinery, sometimes not at all.

Pubs now had to close for a few hours after lunchtime and reopen when the factories closed at tea-time, unbelievably these opening times remained law right up to the late eighties, when the 1988 Licensing Act was introduced.

However, much more draconian measures were to be introduced at the outbreak of World War 1 in 1914. Opening hours were vastly reduced and punters were even urged to not drink on Monday's.

> # Don't Take Alcoholic Drinks on
> # MONDAYS.
>
> In view of the great sacrifices freely made by our sailors and soldiers, the National Organizing Committee feels sure that all who remain at home will willingly help the Country in this way.

But there was more, in 1915, Lloyd George, the Minister for Munitions (and possibly an abstainer from alcohol) said; "We are fighting Germans, Austrians and drink, and so far as I can see the greatest of these deadly foes is drink". There were, possibly some well-founded concerns about alcohols effect on the war effort with it being blamed for productivity and in turn worries of a starvation of ammunition to the overseas troops.

At the very start of the war the Defence of the Realm Act was introduced in an attempt to alleviate some of these concerns. The opening hours were reduced and it was now illegal to buy drinks on credit and also to enter into a round with other people. Unbelievably landlords were even ordered to water down Beer to reduce its strength and cut down on drunkenness!

THE H.J. HULKS ERA

Henry Joe Hulks purchased the Railway Hotel from Emily Collyer in October 1917, and whilst it may seem a strange time to buy such a business with the country still at war, there were to be no shortage of interested parties.

Mr Hulks, known widely as Joe was born c1875 and for many years was also the proprietor of The Kings Head Hotel on Harrow on the Hill, with the family eventually going on to own another four such properties in the local area. Joe had served in the Army during the First World War, having previously been married to Mary who died in or around 1910. Mary was born in 1870 and was previously married with her former married name being, Hefferman. Mary Hefferman's previous husband looks to have died shortly after the couple had a daughter, Margaret born in 1891. Before moving to Harrow Joe Hulks ran a thriving Laundry business in the Bloomsbury area of London, and around the turn of the century married Mary. Margaret, although Joe's stepdaughter, was always treated as nothing other than one of his own family, and although she never took on the name of Hulks both regarded each other as father and daughter!

Joe and Mary had their own son when Henry Joseph Hulks (known as Ted, presumably to avoid the confusion with his father's name) was born in 1901, although there was possibly another son who may have died, as a niece Joy Hulks appears to have been bought up by her auntie Margaret.

WATERED DOWN DRINK AT THE RAILWAY?

After the war had ended Licensing Laws returned to something like normality, it was now not permissible to water down alcohol anymore, in fact the practice so recently encouraged by the Government was now so serious that a big fine and a loss of liberty were some of the tools at the local magistrates disposal. In 1919 Joe Hulks enjoyed the resurgence of his income as Public Houses led the way back to normality for the war weary people of Wealdstone and Harrow. However, it would seem though, that Mr Hulks had made himself some enemies in the locale and his name and honour was bought into question, with rumours that he not only watered down his stock but attempted to bribe the Harrow Observer to stop such a claim appearing within their pages. Rumours were abounding as to where these claims had emanated from, with former disgruntled customers, and fellow local publicans high up on the list. Whoever the culprit was these accusations would not go away, and the Police became involved. Samples of stock were removed for analysis by experts, with nothing untoward being found. Mr Hulks was still far from happy and not only took out the following advert in the local press, but offered a reward to be donated to the Harrow Cottage Hospital. The reward of £50 (somewhere in the region of £580 in today's money) was never claimed with the rumours eventually dying down and Mr Hulks reputation fully restored!

FINED £500 OR SIX MONTHS.

H. J. HULKS, proprietor of the Railway Hotel, Wealdstone, emphatically contradicts the above persistent rumour which has gained currency lately. He offers a reward of

£50 to the Harrow Cottage Hospital

to secure the conviction of the person or persons who have been spreading this rumour.

The taking of samples at his house is quite ordinary to all publicans who open their front doors to police supervision. He likewise begs to state that if he has anything to sell he opens the whole house. He also wishes to refute the rumour that he offered money to bribe the "Harrow Observer" to keep the case out of of that paper.

N.B.—The samples taken by the police were found, on analysis, to be over the required strength.

The Railway hotel at the time had generous stabling facilities, which were now being used less and less. Joe Hulks very soon started to realise the potential of the land and opened a garage, the Railway Hotel Garage was primarily run by Ted Hulks and was soon thriving. Customers could not only buy vehicles they could also rent them as well as having their own repaired. A small haulage service was also offered by the garage which appears to have run for around ten years, by which time the competition in the area made it unviable. In 1921 a small taxi firm was also incorporated for a while into the business, in partnership with Mr J. Cordwell, the venture did not appear to have had a very long life!

Railway Hotel Garage,

'Phone: HARROW 459.

CARS for HIRE

(OPEN AND CLOSED).

LONG DISTANCES A SPECIALITY.
Afternoon Trips arranged.
CARS BOUGHT AND SOLD.

NOTE ADDRESS:
Railway Hotel, Wealdstone.

THE ORDER OFFICE

connected with the
- above Hotel is -

NOW OPEN.

All Orders for Bottled
Ales and Stouts receive
prompt attention.

All kinds of Wines in Stock, the price of which is greatly reduced.

The Railway Hotel Garage & Motor Works

WEALDSTONE, HARROW.

Telephone: HARROW 459.

Proprietors:
H. J. HULKS AND SON.

THE FOLLOWING

Cars in Stock and For Sale:

	£
30 h.p. Brooke Landaulette, 1917	550
15 h.p. Napier Landaulette	345
16/22 h.p. Napier Chassis, Cantilever Springs, Twin back wheels, 1916... ...	450
16/22 h.p. Napier Chassis, Cantilever Springs, single back Wheels, 1917 ...	475
15 h.p. Napier Van, 1 ton ...	195

All the above Cars are in first-class running order, and trial runs can be arranged.

Motor Cars Bought and Sold.
MOTOR CARS FOR HIRE.
PETROL, OIL AND ACCESSORIES kept in stock.

A COUPLE OF ADVERTS FOR THE NEW VENTURE AT THE RAILWAY HOTEL 1919

With two Hotels in the family business a company by the name of H.J.Hulks Limited was setup, with Margaret and Ted both being groomed for a career in the licensing trade, Joe Hulks clearly had his eyes firmly set on continuing to grow his little empire. Around this time Joe also married Alma who would live with him and Margaret at the Kings Head, whilst Ted was ensconced at the Railway Hotel.

In 1920 grand plans were submitted for the first major work on the Railway Hotel since it was built almost seventy years before. However, this was to be a far from easy task to compete, with the country still recovering from the ravages of war, builders were at a premium, and required for what was deemed to be essential work. Many such plans were not approved around this time with priority being given to housing in most cases. The plans were lodged in early 1920 and initially refused, but when resubmitted in April of the same year they were given the green light. The following letter was included in the Harrow Observer urging the council to change their mind:-

RAILWAY HOTEL HALL.

TO THE EDITOR OF THE "OBSERVER."

Sir,—Wealdstone Council, by a small majority, referred back the plans for alteration of the Railway Hotel, which I think would have been a big asset to the residents of Wealdstone. The reasons for this statement are: There are no assembly rooms in the neighbourhood; there are no houses that cater for luncheons for saloon and public-bar customers; there is no billiard room with two tables, the present one at the Railway Hotel being extensively used by discharged soldiers; there is no room in the neighbourhood where clubs' or firms' or private suppers are served (for such as Waterlow's, Kodak, and Winsor and Newton, who have to go out of the neighbourhood when they earn their money to be catered for); and, lastly, the amount of money that will be spent in Wealdstone would be about £7000 to £8000 pounds.

It is suggested that a Wealdstone builder should do the work; therefore Wealdstone men would be employed. For these reasons I think the Council were ill-advised to refer the plans back.

I am, Sir, yours faithfully,
RESIDENT.

Wealdstone, March 20, 1920.

The big-guns from Watney Coombe Reid brewery and Joe Hulks legal team were all present to plead the necessity of these works to be allowed. Having refused the previous application on the grounds that it would be detrimental to the councils housing scheme the meeting which took place at the old council headquarters in Peel Road was told that these works were vital for the following reasons:-

1. A new luncheon and dining room would be included, as well as a workers dining room. There was no such in Wealdstone except for a very small coffee house.

2. There was no venue within the Wealdstone area capable of holding a banquet or a formal dinner.

3. The amount of labour and material required would be relatively small, and would have little or no effect on the provision of dwellings in the district.

Mr Hatton the solicitor representing Watney's and H.J.Hulks Limited made the following representation:-

WEALDSTONE'S NEED.

Mr. Hatton, in opening his remarks, said the scheme was not one which would provide increased facilities for drinking on the premises, and if it did it would be matter for the Licensing Justices. They proposed to provide an adequate service for the provision of meals in the district. It was an extraordinary thing to him that Wealdstone possessed no adequate place at all where meals could be had. He understood there was just a small confectioner's and a small coffee shop or eating house. There were only two fully-licensed houses in the place—the Railway Hotel and the Queen's Arms—and neither had facilities for providing meals, although a licensed house should be a house that provided food and other refreshments for passers by. They proposed to erect a dining and luncheon room, a working man's dining room, and a tea room. His clients were most prominent among brewers in transforming their houses from mere drinking shops to houses where due provision of meals for every class of the community could be decently and properly made. They had embarked on similar large and expensive schemes in the past in various parts of the country, and that was what they wanted to do in Wealdstone. A material part of the scheme applied to the provision of a concert hall. He understood that in Wealdstone there was no concert hall generally available to the public except that which formed part of the Railway Hotel. That hall accommodated about 85 people, but they could not put that number there now without the certainty of an accident, unless they took steps to prop up that part of the building. The hall proposed would hold 200 people, and would be a suitable and pleasant hall for social purposes. By building a concert hall they would be supplying a crying need in the neighbourhood. The Council's housing scheme, he understood, was at present in being only so far as the provision of 14 bungalows was concerned. These bungalows were being erected under contract by a local builder, not not one of the dozen other local builders was engaged on any kind of housing work. Whether his clients did their work or not, the building of the Council's bungalows would be proceeded with and completed. The rest of the Council's scheme was in embryo, and no actual work would be done under it for ten or twelve months. He guaranteed that if his clients were allowed to proceed with their scheme it would be wholly and entirely finished within nine months from that night, so that it would not interfere with the housing scheme. He urged the Council to re-consider their decision to make an order under the Housing Act.

The council were also informed that in any case immediate remedial work would be required to repair the decaying side of the present concert hall as it was in an unsafe state. Mr Hatton said if the new works were refused it would either have to be pulled down or it would fall down! The council were left with very little option but to let the work happen and work commenced very soon after. The concert hall which was suitable for functions of 85 people maximum could now accommodate 200+. The work cost around £8000 to complete and was to change the look of the Railway Hotel for good; it would transform it into a venue suitable for larger music events, and was a decision that was to one day put the venue well and truly on the map!

The work carried out was to basically put a square shaped extension on to the Harrow side of the building, incorporating a new entrance and stage area as well as a dance floor. Aesthetically it was not the greatest of jobs and did little to enhance the fine looking building in any way, and looked particularly ropey from the rear of the building. That aside, it was a much needed addition and one that if it had not happened may well have signalled a very different future for the Railway Hotel.

With the new increased capacity the Railway Hotel's concert hall very soon become a venue for all sorts of local institutions including the local lodge of the Masons of whom Joe was a member. Around this time Joe married Alma who was to be his wife until her death c1932; Alma appears to have been welcomed warmly into the family and was by all accounts quite an accomplished singer! The Hulks family were known to have supported many charities and came together around this time to support a local charity for the Blind. A grand function in the new hall at the Railway featured both Alma and Ted in fine singing voice, and a considerable sum was raised, boosted no doubt by the auction of a live pig which was re-auctioned over a dozen times on the night!

THE HEADSTONE HOTEL

In 1929 a new name was added to the H.J.Hulks Empire, the Headstone Hotel in North Harrow, a brand new purpose built hostelry right opposite the tube station. With Ted more or less running things back at the Railway Hotel it was deemed that Margaret should be the licensee of this exciting new project. Margaret at the time continued to live in the family residence at the Kings Head, but around 1934 was to marry Henry Joseph (another one!) Akam and move to a house near the Headstone Hotel before moving into the property permanently a few years later. Henry was a retired Naval Officer, who served with distinction during the First World War and appears to have had little to do with the running of the Headstone, sadly he and Margaret had a brief marriage as he died in 1942.

All the while Margaret continued to oversee the welfare of her niece Joy who herself was being groomed for a bigger role in the future, in 1953 Margaret and Joy added the Byron Wine Stores to their portfolio and were joint licensees. When Joy went on to marry local man, Douglas Hitchman in 1963 the couple were made managers, whilst Margaret retained her role as licensee.

THE HEADSTONE HOTEL c1970

In 1969 an offer was made to purchase the lease by the brewery Watney Mann, and in early 1970 Margaret moved with Joy and Douglas to The Wheatsheaf Inn, in Grayswood near Hazelmere, Surrey, having purchased the Freehold. Fast approaching her eightieth year she had held the licence at the Headstone for an incredible 41years! It would appear that the new pub in Surrey was an equal success as she was still there at the time of her death in 1988 at the ripe old age of 97! No doubt she would have been less than pleased to have heard about the demise of her former business at the Headstone Hotel which was demolished to make way for flats in 1986. As for Joy, it appears she stayed at the Wheatsheaf for a few more years and died around 2010, the current owner of the pub Ken bought the pub in the late nineties, so obviously something about the lovely old place makes it very hard for people to leave!

In 1935 having recently added an off-licence to the company, and having suffered the recent death of his second wife Joe Hulks died after a short illness at just sixty years of age! H.J.Hulks Limited was split in to two companies, H.J.Hulks (Hendon) Limited and H.J.Hulks (Wealdstone) Limited.

Ted Hulks was by now living in Hendon with his wife Winifred 'Winnie' and went on to have three children, Anthony, Jeanne and Antoinette. With the company soon adding yet another Pub, The Whittington in Pinner to its portfolio Ted and Winnie led a busy life. Things must have been going well for them though, as the big house that they had in Hendon had its own Nanny and Domestic. With Margaret very hands on over at the Headstone Hotel, Ted would rely on trusted management teams to deal with the day to day running of both the Railway and Whittington.

ANOTHER WORLD WAR!

Of course there was also the little matter of another World War looming in the very near future. On 1st September 1939 Hitler's army invaded Poland, very soon after the United Kingdom and France declared War on Germany. Hostilities were to continue for just over six years until VJ day in September 1945. Unlike the First World War Public Houses were now regarded as a vital part of the country's war effort. No more watered down Beer, and during some very grim days for the UK a much needed respite from the seemingly endless hostilities.

With its close proximity to central London, and a major railway connecting it to the north and midlands running straight through it, Wealdstone was a prime target for the German air force. Although, no direct hits are recorded against the Railway Hotel there were to be many highly explosive attacks very nearby, including the total flattening of the Barclays Bank just along the High Street on a particularly busy night of bombing over London in August 1940.

With many men being conscripted, and women being retrained for various other jobs, finding staff for pubs and hotels would prove to be extremely challenging, the advert below was posted in various parts of the country, this one hales from the local publication in Bexhill-on-sea.

> STAFF wanted, suburban district.—Bar-cellarman, barman, barmaid, lounge waiters; good wages and outings; state wages required.—Apply H. J. Hulks, Ltd., Railway Hotel, Wealdstone, Harrow.

With Harrow and Wealdstone station a busy entity for departing and returning servicemen, the Railway Hotel saw its fair share of them tasting their last, or first drink for a while. Also with many Allied forces stationed nearby, in particular Americans they too were made to feel more than welcome, and an effort was made to keep things as near normal as possible, there were regular Dances held in the downstairs ballroom, with the following flyer promoting one such event in early 1945.

> **RAILWAY HOTEL**
> **WEALDSTONE**
> ★
> **DANCING**
> EVERY
> **WEDNESDAY**
> ★ Allied Forces Welcomed ★

When the war finished the UK announced a major house building programme in 1947 and as part of this there was plans to completely redevelop the area in and around Marlborough Hill and other land the Harrow side of the Railway Hotel. Many dilapidated properties were to be hit with compulsory purchase orders, and for a while there were rumours that the Railway Hotel was also going to be knocked down. However, eventually it was deemed that the Railway Hotel was set well back from the highway and 'not obsolete'.

RAILWAY DISASTER

It was precisely 8.19 am on 8th October 1952 (rush-hour) and possibly staff of The Railway Hotel were starting to prepare for opening in a few hours' time, totally oblivious of what was about to happen just a few yards away!

An overnight express train from Perth failed to heed a danger signal prior to entering the confines of Harrow and Wealdstone station at great speed, and subsequently hit the rear of a local service train standing idle. The local passenger service from Tring to Euston at platform 4 was as usual packed with many people standing in the aisles. The force of the impact saw wreckage strewn over the neighbouring tracks and very soon after was hit by a northern-bound express train travelling at around 60 mph. The impact was felt to such an extent that the Railway Hotel was said to have shaken as if hit by an earth quake. The station clock stopped grimly at the exact time of impact as the noise of mangled metal and screams of the injured rang loudly in the air!

The carnage was to claim the lives of 112 people (all but four of which were aged between 15 and 24), with a further 340 injured, some of which were life changing.

Alan Couch Life-Member and a stalwart of Wealdstone Football Club for well over half of a century recalls how his late brother Roy (another fine servant to the club) had a very lucky escape that day;

'At that time we all lived in Hartford Avenue in Kenton and my father and Roy both went to work by train, by first of all catching a 230 bus along Christchurch Avenue to either Kenton Station or Wealdstone whichever one came first. On this particular morning, my father caught the bus to Kenton and was on Kenton Station when the crash happened.

Roy, who just missed the Kenton bus, caught the bus to Wealdstone and the 230 bus was proceeding along Masons Avenue into Wealdstone as the crash occurred and saw the mayhem. A couple of minutes earlier and he would have most likely been crossing the bridge over the platforms. It was such a shock seeing the carnage that he went straight home and didn't go into work. A near neighbour of ours in Hartford Avenue was on the platform and was killed.'

The local rescue services and community quickly mobilised to help the still trapped passengers and injured with first-aid.

The Railway Hotel, also very quickly stepped up to the plate with refreshments and aid being offered to those who were faced with the grim task of dealing with the situation.

The function room which had seen many happy times in its life, was however to see it's saddest that fateful day! The proximity to the crash scene and its external rear doors made it a suitable location to carry the dead into what was to very quickly become a makeshift mortuary.

Whether you believe in these things or not, one thing that could be said with certainty was there have been many accounts of eerie and strange presences in this area, with some claiming it to be haunted by some of the sad soles who lost their lives that day!

THE CARNAGE THAT HAPPENED IN THE WORST PEACE-TIME RAILWAY DISASTER IN THE U.K. – THE RAILWAY HOTEL IS VISIBLE TOP LEFT

ANOTHER PHOTO SHOWING THE DISASTER WITH THE RAILWAY HOTEL TOP RIGHT – NOTE THE SHOPS TO THE RIGHT OF BUILDING

THE WHITTINGTON HOTEL.

As mentioned previously, The Whittington Hotel had now been added to the Hulk's dynasty and was to become a very important and lucrative addition to its portfolio. Although, predictably it would also come with the associated problems of running such a business!

WHITTINGTON HOTEL

Cannon Lane, Pinner

Have you tried us for Functions?

We Specialise in

WEDDING BREAKFASTS

BANQUETS & BUFFETS

H. J. HULKS LTD.   Telephone: PINNER 5688

In 1950, the manager disappeared after accounting discrepancies, taking five years to be tracked down in another part of London; the amount of £124.00 was repaid courtesy of a visit to court! It seems a few years later Ted Hulks good nature was abused again by a retired jockey as detailed in the following local newspaper report.

VANISHED WITH HOTEL 'TAKINGS'

SHORTLY after an ex-professional jockey had been released from prison, he went to the manager of a Pinner hotel, told him of his past and asked him for a job, it was stated at Harrow Court on Tuesday. He was given work as a cellarman and proved to be such a good worker that his wages were increased and he was given a position of trust.

But, the magistrates were told, when the man, Edward Herbert Hack (35), of no fixed address, was sent to the bank with the hotel's takings, on March 9, nothing more was seen of him for more than two months.

After he had pleaded guilty to a charge of stealing a case containing cash and postal orders valued at £211, the property of H. J. Hulks Ltd., proprietors of the Whittington Hotel, Pinner, Hack was committed to Middlesex Sessions for sentence.

D.s. C. Spear told the court that when the accused was seen at Pinner police station on May 31 and was questioned about the money, he replied, "I went up North and lost it racing." None of the money, said D.s. Spear, had been recovered.

THE OBSERVER AND GAZETTE, THURSDAY, JUNE 13, 1957

In the fifties licensing laws were still being strictly applied, but clever landlords were finding their way around them by introducing eateries, whereby you could consume alcohol if you were dining. In 1956 the Whittington came under investigation from the law, with a stiff rebuke and warnings of what would happen if it occurred again. However, two years later following three nights of observation by plain clothed policemen a raid was carried out on the premises!

Ted Hulks and his manager, Edward Lamerton were both summoned to appear in court for 'supplying intoxicating liquor during the supper hour, other than for consumption at a meal supplied at the same time'.

Both men pleaded not guilty and argued that those drinking were also eating sandwiches, after much debate as to whether or not this constituted a meal both were found guilty! Ted Hulks was fined £52 with his manager receiving a fine for £44. A year later in 1959 Ted Hulks decided to give his newly married Daughter Jeanne a unique wedding present, when he handed her over the keys to the Whittington Hotel. Jeanne and her husband Frank were to remain at the Whittington Hotel until 1962, when it was sold to K.W. Jeffreys. Having built up a very good reputation as a wedding reception venue, Frank had also been installed as chairman of the local Licensed Victuallers Association. Frank and Jeanne later went onto have a spell as managers of the Leefe Robinson.

> ## Public house as wedding present
>
> A WELL-KNOWN publican told Gore Division licensing justices on Monday that he wanted to give his 24-year-old daughter and her husband a public house as a wedding present.
>
> He was Henry James Hulks, licensee of The Whittington, Cannon-lane, and he asked for transfer of the licence to Frank and Jeanne Mary Stamp.
>
> "Are you asking for our blessing in this case," said the chairman, Mr. T. N. Graham.
>
> "Your blessing and the transfer," said Mr. A. H. Copley, representing Mr. Hulks.
>
> "We agree and wish them every happiness," said Mr. Graham. "I think that is the proper thing to say in this case."

Now part of the Greene King Meet & Eat brand the Whittington was renamed the Pinner Arms in 2002, with a fine reputation as a good place to eat!

THE LEEFE ROBINSON

In 1948, Ted Hulks on behalf of H.J.Hulks (Hendon) Ltd purchased some land on the corner of Brockhurst corner, and Uxbridge Road from Mr Rackhams a local and well known landowner. Very soon after he submitted plans for permission to build a public house and applied for a joint licence with Winifred to supply intoxicating liquids. It was, ultimately to be an ambition that would take a few years to realise. Indeed, it was some four years before a temporary building with a brick frontage was allowed on the site, with an initial five year approval being granted after much toing and froing!

The project was sold as more of a community centre type establishment than an out and out public house. This appears to have done very little to appease the other local establishments, with the Duck in the Pond, the Seven Balls, the Alma and the Abercorn Arms all lodging their objections. Eventually in June 1954 the new pub was opened and was to be named after one of the local areas heroes.

THE ORIGINAL LEEFE ROBINSON PUB – A PRE-FABRICATED BUILDING WITH A BRICK FRONTAGE

William Leefe Robinson VC was born in 1895, and died at just 23 years of age in December 1918. Leefe Robinson became the first British pilot to shoot down a German airship over Britain during the First World War and was subsequently awarded the Victoria Cross (VC) the first person to be awarded it for action in the UK. Leefe Robinson had been staying at his sister's house in Stanmore where he passed away at the tragically young age having contracted Spanish Flu. Leefe Robinson was to be buried at the nearby Harrow Weald cemetery in a ceremony that bought the local streets to a complete standstill! He was somewhat of a local hero, in particular to Ted Hulks.

NAMED AFTER FLYING HERO

Opening of The Leefe Robinson

The first new public house to be built in Harrow or Wembley since the war, The Leefe Robinson, a pre-fabricated building at Brockhurst Corner, Uxbridge-road, Harrow Weald, was informally opened on Monday evening.

For the proprietors, Mr. and Mrs. H. J. Hulks, it was a triple celebration. It was their 28th wedding anniversary and Mr. Hulks' 53rd birthday.

LUXURIOUS ROOMS

Apart from the handsome brick front, the building is the pre-fabricated hut of familiar kind. Inside, however, things are vastly different. In the two luxurious rooms, "Kite's Bar" and "The Cockpit," furnishings are brilliantly coloured and of ultra-modern design. Clearly there is no intention of the premises being a "local" in the ordinary sense and there is no "saloon" or "public" bar.

Eventually murals will depict the shooting down of the first zeppelin by Lieut. William Leefe Robinson, V.C., in 1916. He died in 1918 and is buried in Harrow Weald cemetery, nearly opposite the building which now, with Air Ministry approval, commemorates him.

THE HARROW OBSERVER DATED 24TH JUNE 1954 DETAILS THE OPENING NIGHT

WILLIAM LEEFE ROBINSON VC. PICTURED DURING WORLD WAR 1

Just over a year after its opening an emotional visit was made by Major E. Leefe Robinson to the establishment that was named after his brother. A dinner was held in the major's honour before a visit to his nearby grave.

At the time Ted Hulks' daughter Jean and her husband, Frank Stamp were managing the family's new addition, and although still a sister pub to the Railway Hotel, Margaret Akam appears to have had nothing to do with the Leefe Robinson.

It was clear that Ted Hulks had other plans for this site and attempted to build a permanent Pub/Restaurant with flats above it. However, these were, predictably knocked back too. Possibly disgruntled and frustrated at being unable to see his vision through Ted decided to put the building up for auction in April 1961, whether there was no interest or he changed his mind is not known. However, the following year Ted Hulks would realise his dream of demolishing the prefabricated building and rebuilding a new permanent structure to consist of a restaurant, two bars, a lounge and a terrace. The work took almost a year to complete and cost in excess of £40,000.

In 2009 the Leefe Robinson was taken over by Miller and Carter who quickly renamed it, however following uproar from local residents it was soon restored back to the original name of the illustrious hero it was named after. Ted Hulks would no doubt have been happy that the tribute to his hero is still thriving!

BACK TO THE RAILWAY HOTEL

With the country still recovering from the trials and tribulations of the recent war, and a few things still on ration, times were tough for many, but there were substantial opportunities for people who were not scared of a hard day's work.

A SIGN LIKE THE ABOVE WAS NOT A RARE SITE IN SOME BRITISH BOARDING HOUSES

Between 1948 and 1970 almost half a million people left the West Indies to live in Britain. The West Indies consists of more than 20 islands in the Caribbean, including Jamaica, Barbados and Trinidad. Many West Indians arrived in the West London area intent on starting a new life, there was also a large influx from India many of whom settled in or around the Harrow area.

Harrow, and Wealdstone in particular, had always been a popular place for Irish people seeking a new life, with times tough back in the homeland, the UK was seen as many as the land of opportunity, however, as you will see from the previous picture the welcome was not always the warmest!

As far back as 1896 people had been making the trip across the Irish Sea, when a Belfast based printing firm by the name of David Allens (later to become Her Majesty's Stationery Office) moved lock stock and barrel to Wealdstone. Many of its employees (my Great-Grandfather and his brother amongst them – and living in nearby Herga Road it's a fair bet that they were the first members of my family to have paid a visit to the Railway Hotel!) moved with them.

It was however, the fifties, sixties and seventies that was to see the majority of Wealdstone's Irish community arrive, with the Railway Hotel soon becoming a home from home for many! Although the Headstone, Whittington and Leefe Robinson were possibly trying to chase a different type of trade, the Railway Hotel was fast becoming very busy traditional pub and quickly gaining a reputation as a music venue, with trad-jazz events as well as the emerging Rhythm and Blues scenes being catered for. The traditional Irish music scene was also starting to be heard within the walls of the Railway Hotel. The Railway Hotel also continued to cater for the wedding trade as well as various other banquets and functions with the following flyer dating back to 1954.

For a Pleasant Evening

with Confidence

either
BANQUETS
• • •
MASONIC LADIES' FESTIVALS
• • •
WEDDING RECEPTIONS
• • •
CLUB DINNERS
• • •
PARTY DANCES
• • •

THERE IS ONLY ONE PLACE

BOOK NOW for the Winter Season
Full particulars from the Manager

RAILWAY HOTEL
PHONE HARROW **0349**　　**WEALDSTONE**

With Ted and Margaret both busy at the company's other outlets it appears that they were having to rely on various Management teams during this period, including Mr and Mrs Clements who ran things at the Railway from 1947 until around 1950. The Railway was still chasing the lucrative wedding and functions market and in 1957 with Margaret taking a more hands on approach the downstairs hall was completely redecorated. One wedding around this time saw two well-known guests in attendance Bond Girl, Shirley Eaton who grew up in Wealdstone was joined by her friend the legendary Max Bygraves. It's not known if Max serenaded the newly married couple on the night – but highly likely!

RAILWAY HOTEL
WEALDSTONE
(PROP.: MRS. M. F. ADAMS)

Newly Decorated Ballroom and Cocktail Bar Now Open for Winter Season Bookings

♦ Banquets　　♦ Private Parties
♦ Buffet Dances　　♦ Wedding Receptions

Apply to the Manager,
Telephone: Harrow 0459

ABOVE A FLYER FROM 1957 ADVERTISING THE NEWLY DECORATED RAILWAY HOTEL'S FUNCTION ROOM AND NEXT AN ADVERT FROM THE HARROW OBSERVER FROM THE FOLLOWING YEAR

H. J. Hulks Limited announce that they have first class facilities for weddings, dinners, dances and other functions at the following hotels:-

"THE HEADSTONE HOTEL"
NORTH HARROW
Telephone Harrow 3321
Catering for up to 250 persons

"THE WHITTINGTON HOTEL"
CANNON LANE PINNER
Telephone Pinner 5688
Catering for up to 120 persons

"THE RAILWAY HOTEL"
WEALDSTONE
Telephone Harrow 0459
Catering for up to 120 persons

Our Managers invite inquiries by telephone or personal call

The Railway going into the sixties was fast becoming better known as a pub and a music venue with the other functions that were once a mainstay happening less and less! To oversee the new direction that the Railway Hotel was heading in a trusted lieutenant was installed in the form of Mr E.H. Hollis who along with his wife had run various pubs in and around London. Well known to Margaret Akam through their connections with the Licensed Victuallers Association they had even held their recent silver wedding anniversary over at the Headstone Hotel. Taking up the post in 1962 it appears they remained at the Railway Hotel until around 1965.

Around this period there was often live music up to four times a week, with other functions such as weddings becoming more and more infrequent, also the off licence was completely scaled down, but nearby in Byron Road Margaret still owned one independent of the H.J.Hulks Company. It was a golden time in the pubs history with packed bars upstairs, and full houses downstairs in the function rooms for the likes of the newly opened 2 R's club and the Studio 1 jazz club.

RAILWAY HOTEL — WEALDSTONE BRIDGE
THE GRAND OPENING OF
THE TWO R.'s
with THE EXILED
Fully Licensed Bar
Friday, 14th Jan., 1966, and Every Friday, 8-11 p.m.
Bus 158, 114, 18

The Hulks Family also diversified slightly when they bought a racehorse that was named Marwin (an amalgamation of Margaret and Winifred) which went on to win a few races before being sent for stud in Australia. There were though inevitably a growing number of unsavoury problems occurring. Was this the reason the Hulks family sold up? Who knows!

THE OBSERVER AND GAZETTE, THURSDAY, OCTOBER 13, 1960

A PRE-WEDDING PARTY COST IRISHMEN £53 IN FINES

THREE police officers arrested nine Irishmen after an eve-of-wedding party at the Railway Hotel, Wealdstone. Among them were three brothers from one family and two from another, one of the latter having travelled up from Wales to be best man at the wedding.

RAILWAY HOTEL
Adj. Stn., Wealdstone
Every Wed. 7.30-11p.m.
2'- before 8 p.m. 3'- after
The Extravaganza Bandwagoners plus top star Prizes and gifts both above Nights.

AN ADVERT FROM THE LOCAL PRESS IN 1962 FOR A MIDWEEK NIGHT WITH THE EXTRAVAGANZA BANDWAGONERS

A BARMAN SERVING THIRSTY CUSTOMERS DOWNSTAIRS AT THE RAILWAY HOTEL – JULY 1964

ALL CHANGE NEAR THE RAILWAY

With the growing population in Harrow, and the fact that the different departments of the council were dotted in various locations around the borough a decision was made to bring everything under the one roof in a new state of the art Civic Centre. In 1961 the following outline designs were submitted, with the landscape near the Railway Hotel destined to change for ever!

There was talk of a hideous looking glass fronted building perched on stilts, also a mock-Georgian design, as we know around a decade later a very different looking Civic Centre was built.

The Railway Hotel was certainly very much thought of when the initial plans were debated, with one local councillor saying that everything should be done to protect the look of the local area, and do nothing to detract from 'two wonderful features of architecture – the Railway Hotel and Wealdstone Station'

The February 2nd edition of the Architects Journal was less than complimentary with its following condemnation of the plans in an article entitled 'Harrowing Prospects'.

> "If you are a sensitive man you would do well not to look behind the Railway Hotel at Wealdstone, in the not very distant future. Harrow Council has decided to put a civic centre there. And because the town has such a splendid Traditional association, this new centre will, of course, be in the revolting Traditional manner. Unless some of the bright local people get together and fight, just as the residents of neighbouring Stanmore are fighting for the abolishment of neo-classical notions in their district.
>
> "There is still time to stop this absurd piece of keeping-in - keeping - with - nothing - in-particular.

The columnist from the Harrow Observer, Plato, was also somewhat peeved about the plans but for a different reason, claiming that the Railway Hotel would be an eyesore to the new building. The Railway Hotel he rather cuttingly remarked is 'a singularly unhandsome building - consisting of big casement windows, pebble dash and nailed- on half timbering'.

THE SIGNAGE THAT HUNG OUTSIDE THE RAILWAY HOTEL FUNCTION ROOM FOR MANY YEARS

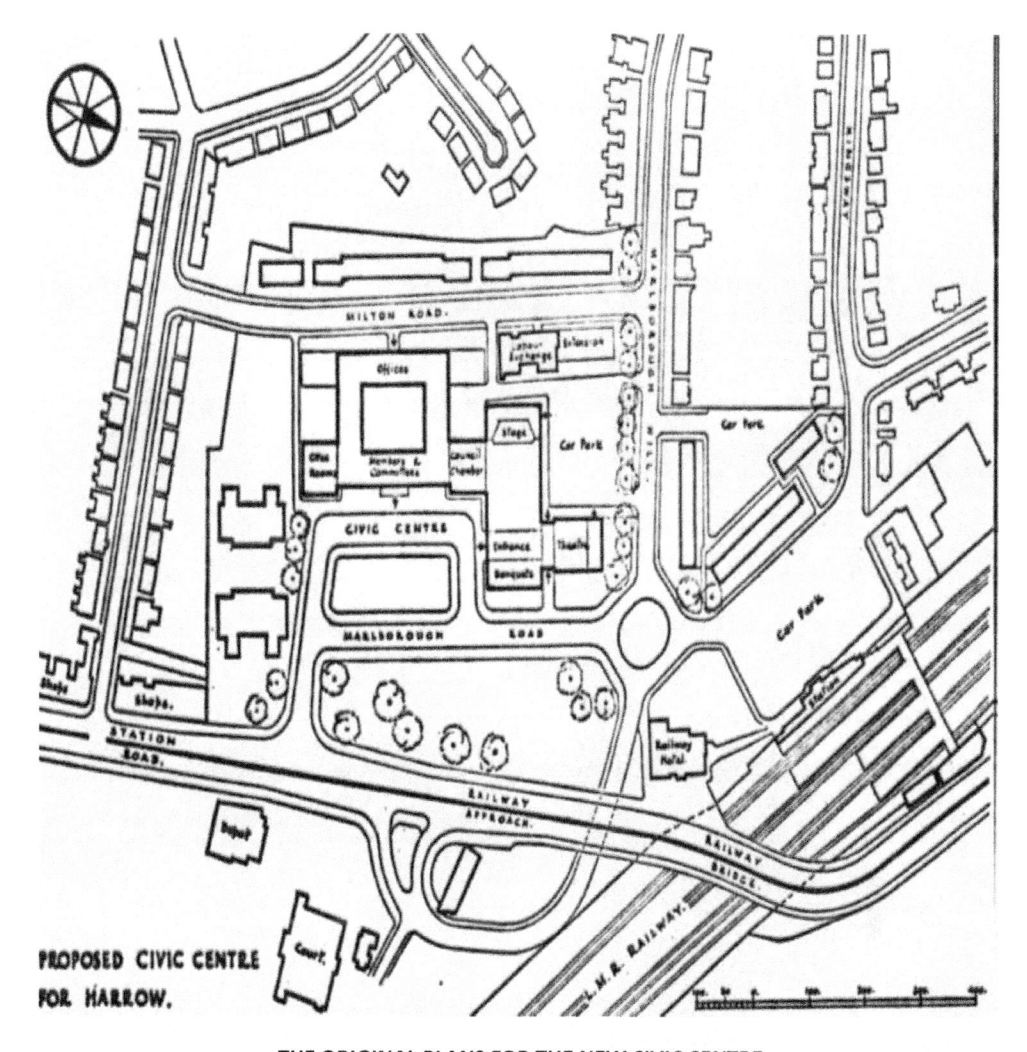

THE ORIGINAL PLANS FOR THE NEW CIVIC CENTRE

It would be a good few years before building work seriously got under way. The previously mentioned shopping parade was a busy and popular entity with everything from tea rooms, hairdressers, cycle shops and a general stores called R.G.JAMES which opened in 1908, and remained until the demolition men moved in some seven decades later!

The shops in the parade were purchased to make way for the new development. The only occupants to refuse all offers were The Wealdstone Social Club and Institute which would remain in situ for another 45 years! The Social Club had been offered the chance to relocate to the nearby Magistrates Court as well as a handsome financial inducement, but the resolute members still refused a fact that was known to have severely peeved the Harrow Council!

STATION APPROACH SHOPPING PARADE IN 1970 JUST PRIOR TO BEING DEMOLISHED – THE RAILWAY HOTEL IS JUST VISIBLE AT THE END

THE FAMOUS R.G.JAMES GENERAL STORE WITH THE PROPRIETORS DAUGHTER OUTSIDE – OPENING ITS DOORS IN 1908 THIS SHOP WOULD REMAIN UNTIL 1970

The Wealdstone Social Club with its neighbouring shops gone had a new neighbour in the form of The Railway Hotel! A close working relationship was always enjoyed between the club and the Railway Hotel, with the later stepping in during World War 2 to help its neighbour when its own hall had been requisitioned by the Army.   For a brief period members were forced to meet in the downstairs hall at the Railway Hotel, so not for the first time it came to the aid of a Wealdstone club!

WEALDSTONE SOCIAL CLUB SHORTLY BEFORE CLOSING IT'S DOORS FOR THE LAST TIME – ANOTHER LOCAL BUILDING CURRENTLY AWAITING DEMOLITION

The shopping parade now gone an underpass was made for easier access to the new Civic Centre, this being parallel with the entrance to the Hotel's entrance in Marlborough Hill at a cost of some £200,000. The land where this underpass would end up (to the side of The Railway Hotel) was still at the time a grassed area. The Civic Centre was officially opened on Sunday 6th May 1973, and at the time of writing is now rather ironically awaiting its own demolition!

THE FLATTENED AREA OF THE SOON TO BE BUILT CIVIC CENTRE ON 2ND JULY 1970 – A COMMEMORATIVE PLAQUE WAS PLACED BY THE MAYOR OF HARROW - (note The Railway Hotel top right in both pictures)

A FEW MONTHS LATER WITH THE WORK WELL UNDER WAY THE RAILWAY HOTEL STILL DOMINATES THE SKYLINE – BUT THIS WOULD NOT LAST FOR MUCH LONGER!

THE UNDERPASS BEING CONSTRUCTED AND ALMOST FINISHED WITH THE RAILWAY HOTEL TOP RIGHT

A NEW ERA!

With a near fifty year dynasty from the Hulks family coming to an end Dugald 'Duggie' Stead and his wife Peggy were installed as the new licensees of the Railway Hotel. Duggie and Peggy had previously been at the Frankfort Arms (now Kenricks Bar) in Paddington for around five years.

> **Mr. & Mrs. DUGALD STEAD**
> of the
> **"FRANKFORT ARMS"**
> 518 Harrow Road, W.9
>
> WISH ALL THEIR MANY CUSTOMERS A
> HAPPY XMAS & A BRIGHT NEW YEAR

During this era one very well-known local man, Maurice 'Morrie' Bush would regularly be seen on the door at the downstairs music events. A former heavyweight boxer, Morrie now made his living as a TV and film extra, appearing in amongst other things Dr.Who, and the first two Star Wars films. A big and well respected man not many people were stupid enough to incur his wrath! But although a tough man, Morrie had a reputation as a gentleman, no more evident than when he organised a fund raising event at the Railway Hotel to assist a local family who suffered a severe tragedy, having lost four children in a house fire. The Bettles family were known to Morrie, and a packed house raised a large sum to help the decimated family set up a new home in another part of the Borough.

MAURICE 'MORRIE' BUSH

In 1968 Duggie Stead found himself in front of the local magistrate's court for allegedly turning a blind eye to gambling and also allowing drunkenness.

Licensee fined on two counts

THE LICENSEE of the Railway Hotel, Wealdstone, was found guilty at Harrow Court on Tuesday of two summonses of permitting drunkenness and gaming on his premises.

Duggie Stead pleaded not guilty on both counts, following a visit by a plain-clothed policeman who said he saw seven men all worse for drink and playing cards for money! Duggie Stead was said to have seen what was going on when he entered the bar to speak to his manager, but chose to ignore it.

For his troubles Duggie Stead was fined £5 on both counts plus £33 8S costs. The manager, Mr McCann who said he was on strict instructions not to allow gambling was not fined, however all of the seven men involved were also charged.

1968 was not a great year for Duggie Stead with the ever-present concerns over violence never seemingly too far away. In December in the space of a few days there were two serious incidents. The first happened when one youth glassed another during a Disco downstairs in the function room, which ended up in court and the next was a totally unprovoked attack which saw an innocent bystander being stabbed in the Railway Hotel's car park.

YOUTH STABBED IN CAR PARK ATTACK BY GANG

Victim an 'innocent bystander'

A 20-YEAR-OLD YOUTH was stabbed in the back outside the Railway Hotel, Wealdstone, on Friday night when he was attacked by a gang of about 20 youths.

The attack came shortly after 11 p.m. when the youth — police do not wish to disclose his name and address for fear of reprisals — and his companion — attempted to drive his open sports car out of the car park.

His way was blocked by a group of about 20 youths. He sounded his horn and they then moved to the car, smashing the windscreen and beating him and his companion about the head and body.

He managed to 'drive off and went into Wealdstone police station to report the incident when it was noticed that the back of his jacket was saturated with blood.

Stitches

A knife wound was found below his right shoulder blade, only an inch or so from his spine.

He was taken to Harrow Hospital where four stitches were inserted. He was detained overnight but was able to leave hospital the following morning.

Police say the youths had been attending the discotheque, housed in the basement of the hotel.

"It was a completely unprovoked attack on an innocent bystander," said a senior officer at Harrow police station.

THE HARROW OBSERVER 10TH DECEMBER 1968

In the New Year with the Friday and Saturday night club nights downstairs suffering a bit from the recent negative publicity, Ray Peterson the organiser went public in a bid to assure people of their safety, assuring potential punters that the Railway club night was a safe place to visit. To be fair the club had only had a handful of minor incidents in little over a year; although this did not stop a full police raid a couple of months previous!

Police eject pregnant woman from pub bar

A HARROW housewife ejected from the Railway Hotel public house by a policeman, was fined £5 by Harrow magistrates on Tuesday.

A BY NOW ALL TOO FAMILIAR INCIDENT AT THE RAILWAY IN SEPTEMBER 1969!

Two jailed for assaulting man in public house

TWO MEN charged with assaulting another man in the Railway Hotel, Wealdstone, causing him grievous bodily harm, received prison sentences of three months at Harrow Court last week.

In the early days of the new decade Duggie Stead was again in court after being assaulted by a young customer who had been barred some time previous, a two year suspended sentence was handed out to the young builder! The incident detailed below was another serious incident at the Railway Hotel, happening in August 1970.

Bottles thrown during fight in dance hall

AFTER a fight at the Railway Hotel, Wealdstone, on Friday night, five youths appeared at Harrow Court on Tuesday.

Everton Anthony Dorman (18) a car polisher, of Craven Park Road, Harlesden, denied threatening behaviour.

Kenneth Manning (19) a panel beater, of Nichol Road, Harlesden, and Junior Harris (18) a trainee electrician, of Villiers Road, Harlesden, at first admitted threatening behaviour and assaulting a police officer, but during the case denied doing so.

Lloyd Roberts (18) a tool setter, of Monks Parks, Tokyngton, denied threatening behaviour and having an offensive weapon, and Errol Harrison Greenaway (21) a tool setter, of Park View, Tokyngton, admitted having an offensive weapon.

P.c. Michael Jones said that he was on plain clothes duty on the side entrance of the hotel's dance hall. At about 11.25 p.m. a fight broke out.

P.c. Jones said he went into the hall and saw Dorman throw a bottle into a group of youths on the other side of the hall. He then saw Dorman make his way out to Marlborough Road, at the rear of the hotel.

Later, he said, he saw Dorman sitting in the front seat of a car with two other youths which was about to leave the car park but was held up by traffic congestion.

P.c. Jones said he ordered the driver of the car to stop and asked Dorman and the other youths to get out.

He was hit

Dorman said that everybody was fighting and throwing bottles in the hall and that he had been hit by one. He said he went outside to the car park and was given a lift in a friend's car. As they were leaving, P.c. Jones stopped the car and asked the youths where they came from. Those that said they came from Harlesden were then asked to get out of the car, said Dorman.

A defence witness said that he did not see Dorman throw any bottles during the fight.

Dorman, said to have had three previous convictions, including a six-month suspended sentence for riotous assembly, was given a one-month sentence to run concurrent with the six months.

P.c. David Manson told the court that bottles were being thrown at the stewards inside the hall and that the fight soon spread outside where there was a group of about 150 youths who were shouting at the group throwing bottles.

He said that he saw Manning and Harris throw bottles and that as he was arresting them, Harris grabbed hold of his arm and Manning hit him in the face.

P.c. Manson was then given assistance by P.c. Michael Reynolds who pulled them both away. They were then taken to Harrow Police Station where Harris said to P.c. Manson when being charged: "Did I assault you?"

Denials

Giving evidence, Manning and Harris denied throwing bottles or assaulting P.c. Manson and said they ran away because they wanted to get away from the fight.

Manning was fined £10 for threatening behaviour and £15 for assaulting P.c. Manson. Harris was fined £10 for threatening, and £20 for the assault charge.

Roberts, who denied he had an offensive weapon, a flick knife, said it had been planted on him. He was put on three years probation for having an offensive weapon and fined £10 for threatening behaviour.

Greenaway admitted having an offensive weapon a table knife, and was fined £20.

Weather cut fete profit

Owing to the generosity of several of the friends of Pinner League of Pity (junior branch of the NSPCC) the disastrous weather on Wednesday last week did not entirely ruin their annual fete, held once again in the Paines Lane garden of Mrs.

After a tough year Duggie Stead was no doubt pleased to see two landmark events pass without incident, confirming that the Railway Hotel still had an important role to play in the local music scene. After six years Screaming Lord Sutch made a triumphant return to a packed house, and Soul legend Ben.E.King also played to a sell-out crowd. King was in the UK to promote his new Greatest Hits LP and agreed to play his only London show at the Railway in November – quite a coup!

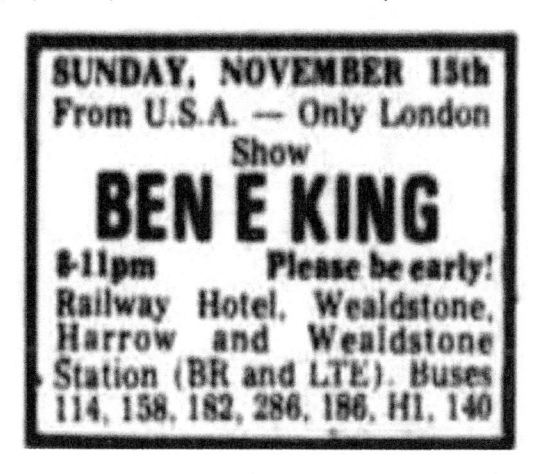

> **SUNDAY, NOVEMBER 15th**
> From U.S.A. — Only London Show
> **BEN E KING**
> 8-11pm   Please be early!
> Railway Hotel, Wealdstone, Harrow and Wealdstone Station (BR and LTE). Buses 114, 158, 182, 286, 186, H1, 140

Sadly the New Year saw the problems return early on with a fight at a wedding, causing the police to attend twice on the one night and charging three of the guests. Later on in the year a gang of youths leaving a disco downstairs attacked a local policeman forcing him to be hospitalised. P.C. David Price was a native of the area and had recently represented Wealdstone Football Club.

P.c. injured in bottle attack

A HARROW police constable who was beaten up by a gang of youths near the Railway Hotel, Wealdstone, on Friday night was "reasonably comfortable" in Mount Vernon Hospital yesterday (Monday).

Duggie Stead must have been getting close to looking elsewhere to make his living, and things would have no doubt been compounded when two of his live-in bar staff were arrested and charged with breaking into various cars in the area and stealing them and their contents, both ended up with prison sentences in excess of six months!

In August 1972 a horrific attack on the doorman downstairs left him needing 72 stitches after being attacked with an axe. The doorman had intervened after an altercation between a man and his girlfriend. The man who was believed to have come from outside the locality was eventually found and charged, resulting in a prison sentence!

HATCHET ATTACK AT DISCO

A steward at the Railway Hotel, Wealdstone, was injured in the chest and arms when he tried to break up a fight between three young people on Sunday night.

One of the youths pulled a hatchet from his pocket as the steward intervened, a police officer told magistrates at Harrow Court on Tuesday.

Later on in the year, more trouble flared at the newly named Kiwi Club in the downstairs function rooms at the Railway Hotel.

THINGS WENT CRAZY AT KIWI CLUB

WHEN POLICE RAIDED the Crazy Kiwi Club at the Railway Hotel, Wealdstone, on Friday, a fracas broke out among several men, Harrow Court heard on Tuesday.

Shortly before he left the Railway Hotel there was a fire when a carelessly discarded cigarette caught a number of beer crates and some fencing alight, a more than eventful time for Duggie Stead came to an end with Thomas O'Neill coming into replace him as a brewery appointed manager. Thomas O'Neill seemingly went in there with a very much 'new broom sweeps clean' attitude as detailed in the local newspaper report below.

Change at Railway

Past trouble at the Railway Hotel, Wealdstone, was recalled by Hendon licensing magistrates on Tuesday.

The chairman, Col. W. D. Morris, said the bench was concerned whether the new licencee, Mr. Thomas O'Neill, could handle the discotheque, where he said, there had been considerable trouble in the past.

He said: "We will grant the transfer of the licence with a very firm piece of advice or warning of what might happen. It is up to you to make sure you stamp out any trouble."

Mr. O'Neill said he had worked in public houses before, and could handle the Railway Hotel. There were no police objections to the transfer.

OBSERVER AND GAZETTE Friday, September 6, 1974

Although a brief tenure (just slightly less than a year), Thomas O'Neill appears to have been true to his word, with a relatively and most welcome quiet period at the Railway during this time. However, there was a major swoop at the nearby station when around fifty youths were arrested on their way to a Disco at the Railway Hotel having avoided paying their fares, which was obviously something that was not within his remit anyway!

In August 1975 John Charles was installed by Watney's as the new manager of the Railway Hotel, with his first task to stop the anti-social behaviour that was happening when people left the downstairs Disco and still carrying their bottles and glasses. An ongoing problem for a while, a strict 'no bottles and glasses outside' rule was implemented! The new rule seemed to have had little impact as it was still being talked about at Harrow Road Safety Council level just a couple of months later!

Bottles ban promise

The new manager of the Railway Hotel, Wealdstone, has promised action to prevent customers littering the area around the pub with broken bottles.

Last week a Harrow Council spokesman told the Observer that the problem of broken glass on the pavement outside the pub, and on the road by the Marlborough Hill underpass, was a "constant headache."

An Observer reader also wrote complaining about broken glass on the steps leading from Marlborough Hill to the Wealdstone bridge.

"The trouble is caused from the dance hall, Railway Hotel, about three times a week. It is very dangerous for the old folk, as well as any child, if they were to fall," the reader, an elderly lady, wrote.

Problem

The council spokesman said: "This area is a constant problem to us, and we keep a close eye on it — as much as we can bearing in mind that we have 250 miles of public highway in the borough to look after."

A council van visited the area every week to clear broken glass from the pavements and road, he added.

Mr. John Charles, who started as manager of the pub three weeks ago, told the Observer that he would be doing his best to prevent the problem happening again.

"We had a problem with this over the weekend," he said. "We spent part of Monday clearing up the pavement ourselves."

Mr. Charles added that customers would not be allowed to take bottles outside the pub in future.

> **COME AND ENJOY YOURSELF AT THE RAILWAY CHRISTMAS DAY**
>
> Opening times: 12 noon till 2 p.m., 7 p.m. till 10.30 p.m.
> DISCO BAR 24th till 12 midnight
> 26th till 12 midnight, 27th till 11 p.m.
> 31st, 12.30 bar 1 p.m. finish.
> Entrance 60p
>
> **THE RAILWAY HOTEL**
> Station Approach,
> Wealdstone, Harrow
> 01-427 0459

AN INVITATION TO THE RAILWAY HOTEL CHRISTMAS 1975

In 1976 it was all change again at the Railway Hotel with St. Georges Taverns adding it to their chain and installing Tom and Sue Spooner as their new management team. St Georges Taverns was a London based company that included the likes of the John Lyon pub in Sudbury Town, and went onto spend a considerable sum on refurbishing the now tired looking old building. A new food bar was added to the premises and re-opened just in time for the 1976 Christmas period. Interestingly the 'Hotel' part of its title was dropped during this period for some reason!

> # THE RAILWAY
>
> **RAILWAY APPROACH, WEALDSTONE**
>
> ## TOM & SUE SPOONER
> announce their re-opening after
> extensive re-decoration
>
> ON
>
> **WEDNESDAY, 15th DECEMBER
> AT 12.30 p.m.**
>
> **FIRST DAY ONLY:-**
> All Spirits: 20p per nip, a free glass of Wine with each meal from our new food bar.
>
> A ST. GEORGES' TAVERN HOUSE.

Around 1978 it would appear that St. Georges Taverns pulled out of the Railway, and managers were again installed by the brewers, Watney's.

TOM & SUE SPOONER welcome you to :—
THE RAILWAY
A ST GEORGES TAVERN
LUNCHEONS · HOT & COLD SNACKS · CAR PARK
STATION APPROACH.
WEALDSTONE, MIDDX.
Phone :
01-427-0459

A 1977 FLYER FOR THE RAILWAY (NOT KNOWN AS THE RAILWAY HOTEL DURING THIS PERIOD)

Following this period there were a number of managers installed by Watney's including Thomas Gallagher, who was replaced by Dennis and Margaret McDonald. The generosity of the customers was again evident in 1980 when a tidy sum was raised for the nearby Firs School for handicapped children.

Beer drinkers aid handicapped

CUSTOMERS at the Railway public house in Wealdstone have raised £220 for the Firs School for the Handicapped in The Heights, Northolt.

The money came from a Country and Western Evening on May 12 during which Watney's Special Bitter was sold at half price.

Bottles of wine, spirits and perfume were raffled and licensees Dennis and Margaret McDonald provided a buffet.

Sadly Dennis McDonald's reign at the Railway was not to end in the way he hoped as detailed below in the Harrow Midweek dated 6th October 1981.

Manager stole cash and drink from pub

By Elizabeth Grun

A FORMER manager of the Railway, Wealdstone, was sentenced to nine months imprisonment suspended for two years on Friday.

Dennis Augustus McDonald, 37, of Beethoven Road, Elstree, appeared at Harrow magistrates court on three theft charges.

He pleaded guilty to stealing £400 cash, bottles of gin, whisky, brandy, rum, Tia Maria, Drambuie and vodka valued at £494 and £1,000 in cash, all from the Railway Tavern and the property of Watneys Breweries.

On each charge he was sentenced to three months imprisonment to run consecutively, suspended for two years. He was also ordered to pay £400 compensation.

Det Sgt Kenneth Macrae, prosecuting, said Mr McDonald stole the cash and alcohol because he was forced to do so.

"Mr McDonald reported a burglary at his public house, but when he was interviewed by the police at length there were suspicious circumstances. Mr McDonald made certain admissions," said Det Sgt Macrae.

"He admitted stealing the cash and alcohol."

Statements were not read in open court but it was explained that Mr McDonald, who had no previous convictions, carried out the thefts because he was under pressure.

"Other men have appeared in court on these matters and were given suspended prison sentences," said Det Sgt Macrae.

Mr Nicholas Crighton, defending, said Mr McDonald had built up good trade at the pub.

"Mr McDonald was subjected to an unpleasant protection racket and he should have gone straight to the police. But he has a weak character and was afraid of what might have happened," said Mr Crighton.

Following on from Dennis McDonald, Watney's again installed various management teams including Tom O'Flaherty until 1982 when Brendan Hipwell took on the lease.

THE WEALDSTONE FOOTBALL CLUB CONNECTION

Given the proximity of Wealdstone Football Club to The Railway Hotel it is perhaps not surprising that the two have had some more than tenuous links over the years.

As early as November 1890, a forerunner to what was to ultimately become the Wealdstone Football Club of today held their first ever benefit concert in the Hotel's function rooms. This came about when a player by the name of Fred Pearce was forced to retire from the game and even render him unemployed due to a severe injury whilst playing for the club. A benefit concert was held with entertainment provided by none other than The Wealdstone Minstrels, featuring many of Fred's ex-team mates!

The Minstrels (not to be confused with the politically incorrect version of the seventies) performed recitals of poetry as well as singing, dancing and generally entertaining the crowd!

The Railway Hotel thereafter became an unofficial headquarters for the club, with meetings being regularly held there, such as an end of season event following the successful campaign of 1892/93 in which they only tasted defeat three times in their nineteen matches. A clarion call was made for all interested parties to attend, as the club were eager to build on their success by introducing a reserve team. At the time other local pubs such as the nearby Queens Arms and The Havelock in Harrow were even used as makeshift changing rooms.

In April of 1895 another meeting at The Railway was held to form a new football club entitled Wealdstone Athletic, an early gestation of what was to become Wealdstone Football Club. This 'strand' of the club was not to enjoy a long life with players leaving the club in their droves due to the appalling state of the playing surface at the time! In 1899/1900 the club was officially named as Wealdstone Football Club, with early games being played literally just up the road in Marlborough Hill, meetings and functions continuing to be held at The Railway; however The Queens Arms was again utilised for changing facilities.

It was in 1905 that Wealdstone were to win their first title when they were crowned as champions of the Willesden and District Football League. A celebration was called for in the form of a Football Club Smoking Concert, again held at The Railway Hotel. A smoking concert was a gentleman only evening where they would be entertained by music, whilst smoking and talking about politics and generally putting the world to rights. This curious event was reported in the Harrow Observer thus:-

'The RAILWAY Hotel was the meeting place of footballers in the district on Saturday night, when Wealdstone Football Club held a most successful smoking concert.

The Chair was occupied by a Mr A Murray, himself a footballer of no mean ability, noted throughout Wealdstone and the neighbourhood as a good half back. Supporting the Chairman were Messrs E.E. Beckley (Hon Secretary), J Harris and G White, whilst in the room could be seen many familiar faces in the football world including Messrs H Bowell, J Brown, Saunders, Gregory, W Carmalt and members of the Wealdstone Church F.C.

The late arrival of the pianist delayed the start, but despite this the concert went from start to finish with smoothness, which was most creditable to the Committee.

The toast of 'The Visitors' was proposed by Mr E.E. Beckley who congratulated the Church F.C on having won the Wembley and District League, and Mr G Elmslie, secretary of the Wealdstone Church F.C., gave a similar courteous reply.

The toast of The Chairman having been drunk with musical honours, Mr Murray proposed Wealdstone Football Club. In a few well-chosen words, he congratulated the club on winning the Championship of the Willesden and District League, not yet having sustained a defeat in that competition.

The vocal items were huge successes, and encores were frequent. The humorous selections naturally claimed most attention and the comedians included such popular favourites as Mr Charlie Sherlock and Mr Harry Jeanes who gave several songs. Mr W.J .Beckley played a capital violin solo and Mt Tit Baldwin showed a wonderful skill with the bones.' (Note the bones were a pair of wooden percussion instruments that were previously made from animal bones.)

The celebratory evening, which was, obviously, very much of its time turned out to be the last of its type for a while at the club, the following season saw the club fall into disarray to such an extent they failed to complete their fixtures. Church Athletic F.C., who had been the clubs guests at the recent event at the Railway Hotel stepped in and completed the season on their behalf!

It was not until the 1908/09 season that a fully independent Wealdstone Football Club was to return to competitive action, having effectively been a club within a club at Church Athletic F.C. Many officials and players had been involved with both entities, the 'new' Wealdstone F.C. began to flourish to such an extent that they actually fielded two separate first teams in different leagues during the 1913/14 season. This season would be the last for five years as very soon after the country were fully embroiled in the First World War. Football returned for the 1919/20 season, and two years later saw the club purchase the freehold of a piece of land called Lower Meadow, some few hundred yards from The Railway Hotel. The club shortened the name to Lower Mead and built its new ground there, remaining at Lower mead for almost seventy years before a disastrous chain of events saw them forced to sell up and move out of the town. As a precursor to the 1949/50 season a special match was played against Schaffhausen FC from Switzerland with a special celebratory dinner held in the function room at the Railway Hotel, the Swiss team is still thriving in its homeland and is now plying its trade in the second tier of their domestic league.

Wealdstone's last league match at Lower Mead was on Saturday 27th April 1991, the end of an era, which was rounded off by a sizeable amount of Stones supporters mourning the loss at The Sidings well into the early hours of the following day!

The Railway Hotel was to come back on to the club's radar in 1994, when an attempt was made to establish an identity back in Harrow. The club having played in Watford, and at the time in Yeading, were suffering from a severe lack of income and looked into the possibility of buying a lease on a Pub or Bar in the local area. The Railway Hotel was one of many potential names mentioned, however almost simultaneously an approach was made to the club from the nearby St. Josephs Social Club. Ultimately, the later never came to anything either and it would be some years before the club had their own bar again, when eventually they took over operations at Ruislip Manor F.C., a move that has thankfully seen them rightfully back in the top echelons of the non-league game.

THE OFFICERS AND COMMITTEE OF THE

Wealdstone Football Club

extend to their guests

SCHAFFHAUSEN F.C.
(Switzerland)

a very warm welcome and
invite them to dinner at the

RAILWAY HOTEL
WEALDSTONE

at 6.0 p.m.

following their match

SATURDAY, AUGUST 27th, 1949

THE DINNER MENU FROM THE PREVIOUSLY MENTIONED MATCH IN 1949

PROMOTE WEALDSTONE F.C.

THE HALF MOON

Alan Carroll

Roxeth Hill,
Harrow

THE RAILWAY HOTEL

Live Bands Every Saturday
The Bridge
Station Approach
Wealdstone

AN ADVERT FROM A WEALDSTONE F.C. PROGRAMME c1994

THE HIPWELL ERA

In 1982 Brendan Hipwell took over the lease of the Railway Hotel, adding it to a portfolio of pubs that the Hulks family would have been more than proud of!

Brendan Hipwell, a well-known publican based in the West London area was also chairman of the Hammersmith & Fulham branch of the Licensed Victuallers Association and had a further four pubs in his chain, one in the City of London, the Crown Inn in Dunstable, The Hop Poles in Hammersmith and the Princess Victoria in Shepherds Bush. When the Railway Hotel was added to the chain, Brendan's brother Derry was the man tasked with running the place, he was assisted by Ron Meredith the deputy-manager, with Derry's wife, Pat and Ron's wife, Sheila taking care of the catering side of the business, which went onto become a busy and lucrative trade, particularly at lunch time! The lunchtime trade was soon booming with the pub being a favourite haunt for employees of the nearby Civic Centre and Magistrates Court. The queues were long and everyday was a sell-out!

Around this time Lucy Challis joined the staff, and was to stay right throughout the Hipwell era, pulling pints at the Railway Hotel for some fifteen years in total! Lucy soon went onto become a well-known figure at the Railway, popular with the staff and customers alike, and was once asked to act as a character witness for a lad called 'Bernie'. Lucy tells the story thus: - 'There was a fight downstairs one night and a lad called Bernie was arrested. Bernie had done nothing so I went as a witness for him. When I went into the magistrate's court to give evidence, there was a lot of whispering, and then the clerk said I couldn't be a witness, as I served them lunch every day! But it worked. They thought if I was willing to vouch for Bernie, he must be okay. He got off'.

LUCY CHALLIS PICTURED WITH PAT HIPWELL AND SHEILA MEREDITH AT THE RAILWAY HOTEL

BUSY LONDON PUBS require (1) Trainee Management, couples, aged 18 to 30. Accom. provided, wages neg. Experience in Bar and Catering essential. (2). Experienced Bar Persons, aged 18 to 25. Accomm. provided, £90 p.w. Please apply (giving details of experience and refs.) to Mr. B. Hipwell, Head Office, C/o The Railway Hotel, Railway Approach, Harrow, HA3, 5BT.

Evening Herald, Tuesday, March 24, 1987   31

Of course the odd scuffle in a Pub is hardly headline news, however during the late eighties there were more than one or two unsavoury incidents happening on an irregular basis. Brendan Hipwell was even assaulted for no apparent reason by somebody with a plank of wood, requiring hospital treatment and twelve stitches. The incident which happened in April 1987 even made the local Thames TV news.

THE LEADER Friday, April 10, 1987

Three coshed at pub
Man goes berserk

A MAN went berserk and coshed three people with a lump of wood after he was thrown out of a private party at The Railway pub in Wealdstone.

The attack followed an earlier assault at the party when landscape gardener Manning Boswell from Farnborough had a beer glass pushed in his face, leaving him with deep cuts to his face and forehead.

Police say that the attacker was among the group who were thrown out of the pub in Station Road for the beer glass incident.

The attacker returned shortly after and hit the licensee Brendan Hipwell, leaving him with a four-inch gash on the forehead.

He then attacked a father and son. Joseph Long Junior, 23, of Austen Road, South Harrow, and 44-year-old carpenter Joseph Long Senior both suffered minor injuries from blows.

Manager Derry Hipwell, 48, says the man hit out indiscriminately during the attack shortly before 1 am.

THE RAILWAY'S CURE FOR A CHRISTMAS HANGOVER!

The Christmas edition of The Harrow Observer in 1987 sought expert advice as how to best alleviate a hangover during the festive period. Stargazer, Russell Grant suggested Eno's and water, however Railway Hotel manager, Derry Hipwell favoured the tried and tested format of a good fry-up the following day! 'Have a damn good fry-up and carry on, that gets rid of the acid that causes a hangover' was Derry's expert opinion, and one that has continued to serve many people, for many years!

● There's nothing like a good breakfast to make those morning after feelings fry away. Derry Hipwell, landlord of The Railway Hotel, in Wealdstone, tucks into his favourite remedy.

In 1988 Derry Hipwell rewarded one of its most loyal customers, Harold Pope free Beer for life. Harold who lived a stone's throw away from the pub had been using it for almost thirty years and was a well-known and popular figure at the Railway Hotel.

Cheers - to a daily free pinta

CHEERS! Beer lover Harold Pope toasts his favourite pub after his loyalty was rewarded with every drinker's dream — free pints for life.

Grandad Harold, 90, of Churchill Place, Wealdstone, has been a regular at The Railway on Wealdstone bridge since 1970.

And landlord Derry Hipwell decided that it was time for him to enjoy a couple of pints on the house each day for the rest of his life.

Harold said: "Obviously, I am very pleased and honoured to be offered free drinks.

It's clear that the Railway's customers and the wider community were important to the Hipwell's, and when regular Mick McManus lost his fight with cancer in 1986, a decision was made to commemorate him at his favourite pub. A collection was organised to raise £150 for a hardwood bench with a memorial plaque for Mick who lost his fight at just 43 years of age. Subsequently the generosity of the Railways locals raised ten times that amount! A decision was quickly made to make a donation to Mount Vernon Hospital.

Hospital gets big boost from the boozer!

FUND-RAISING regulars at the Railway Hotel in Wealdstone have raised £1,400 for cancer patients in memory of one of their drinking mates who died two years ago.

Mick McManus, of Cullington Close, Wealdstone, died of cancer at just 42 and friends of the popular local character were determined to collect as much cash as possible for Mount Vernon Hospital, which nursed him during his last days.

This week, landlords Derry Hipwell and Ron Meredith bought three TV sets, two armchairs and two sophisticated intravenous drug machines for cancer patients at the Northwood hospital after the pub's latest fund-raising efforts.

The hospital's senior manager of the radiotherapy unit, Vicky McIntosh, is pictured with patient Peter England and Mr Hipwell.

Almost in tandem with the above, a generous £1000 was further raised by the regulars for the Great Ormond Street Children's Hospital by means of a huge pile of pennies in the Saloon bar. A towering pile of pennies stood four feet high on the bar, held together by a small dab of Guinness it took just eight weeks to raise the amount!

DERRY HIPWELL WITH SON MICHAEL c1990

Sadly in May 1989 the unsavoury report appeared in the Harrow Leader; however the callous act done nothing to deter the staff and regulars at the Railway Hotel who continued raising huge sums in memory of their departed friend!

Thieves hit new

depths

A FURIOUS pub landlord has put up a £100 reward after thieves stole a bench bought in memory of a cancer-stricken regular.

Landlord Derry Hipwell of The Railway Tavern is determined to retrieve the hardwood park bench and a table which were snatched between last Wednesday or Thursday – and he is offering the reward for its return and information leading to the conviction of the thieves.

Mr Hipwell said: "I wouldn't like to be in the thieves' shoes if the customers ever got hold of them.

We all feel very bitter about what's happened."

The bench was placed at the front of the pub in Station Approach, Wealdstone, with an epitaph to one of the pub's most popular figures Mick McManus.

Mr McManus, who was a widely-known local window cleaner and better known in the pub as an odd-job man, died in June 1986 aged 43 after a long fight against cancer.

After his funeral regulars at the pub set up a fund in his name to raise money in aid of the cancer ward at Mount Vernon Hospital where he was cared for until he died.

The first £150 went towards the memorial bench but since then kind-hearted pub-goers have raised at least £2,000 a year for the hospital.

Mr Hipwell added: "Mick McManus was everybody's friend. If he only had a fiver but you needed it, he would give it to you."

Mr McManus's best friend of 30 years, Martin O'Dwyer said: "Mick and I both suffered from cancer and were treated at the same hospital. The only difference is that he died from it and I survived.

"A lot of time and effort was spent getting the bench for him and the money we've raised is going up and up each year. At least they can't nick that."

● **Flashback.....Railway Tavern assistant manager Ron Meredith (centre) and regulars Den Cronin (left) and Les Watts at the presentation of a bench in memory of Mick McManus.**

In 1995 John Major's Conservative Government decided to repeal the dated Sunday licensing laws, and allowed Pubs to stay open all day; however this was not welcome by all – with even Brendan Hipwell sounding a note of caution in the Kensington Gazette.

Hammersmith & Fulham Licenced Victuallers Association chairman Brendan Hipwell said: "Extended opening hours will suit Soho and West End pubs one hundred per cent.

"But in the local pubs it will ruin that cosy Sunday lunchtime session which is a very traditional part of the day before you go home for lunch.

Despite many people's reservations, not least the church the first Sunday in August 1995 saw pubs up and down the country opening all day for the first time. The old 'sprint to the finish' lunchtime session 12-2pm (later 12-3pm) was now a thing of the past, and punters now had the chance to watch Premier League or Gaelic Football every Sunday, with no doubt ,many Dinners left in the oven, or not touched at all! Of course the Railway Hotel like everywhere soon adapted, and it now seems strange to think that these were at the time quite revolutionary changes.

The late eighties to mid-nineties saw a slump in the construction trade which would later have a major impact on the Railway Hotel. The Pubs within the Hipwell chain would all be affected by the recession, with builders being hit particularly badly, these punters were the pubs chore trade and very much the bread and butter of the business. Lucy Challis recalls the changing times *'The recession hit about 1986 or 1987. The pub trade was really hit. It went on for years; all our customers were in construction, which was hit hard. Many of the rich contractors, who used to buy big rounds, were reduced to maybe a half of lager'.*

THE BAR AT THE RAILWAY HOTEL 1988

In October 1995 following what was described by the Police as 'a substantial increase in the number of drunken, violent incidents' the Sidings had its late licence severely restricted, with closing times capped at Midnight, and only private functions being permitted. This obviously had a major impact on trade, and following a major outcry from punters and even Screaming Lord Sutch an appeal was lodged to be heard by the local magistrate's court in December, which was subsequently adjourned until January 17th 1996. Sutch spoke with passion about his old hunting ground, and even promised to do a special gig on its re-opening!

In a marathon fifteen hour session at the original hearing, evidence was heard from no less than seventeen police officers, three lawyers and two environmental health officers. The main protagonist from the Police, Inspector Spivey claimed that the club attracted 'undesirables and underage drinkers, and that the police had been called to the premises on at least 18 times in the previous year to deal with fights, assaults and drunkenness'. The Railway had also been ordered to improve communication between the basement and main pub to stop customers leaving the premises with glasses and bottles. Brendan Hipwell spoke up for the Railway Hotel and stated that there was not one single complaint from local residents, and therefore the Sidings should be allowed to return to its previous 2.00am licence.

Future of 60s music venue to be decided

THE FUTURE of the famous Sixties music venue in the basement of Wealdstone's Railway Hotel will be decided by magistrates later this month.

Music lovers from across the world used to visit the club where The Who's Pete Townshend first smashed his guitar on stage and rockers Jeff Back, Jimmy Page and Screaming Lord Sutch launched their careers.

But the club in Railway Approach has been closed to all but private functions since October last year after losing its late licence following police claims of "a substantial increase in the number of drunken, violent incidents."

Insp Perry Spivey claimed the club attracted "undesirables" and under-age drinkers and that police had gone to The Railway at least 18 times in the year to deal with fights, assaults and drunkenness.

Evidence was heard from 17 police officers, three lawyers and two environmental health officers during a marathon 15-hour hearing by Harrow Council's public entertainments and licencing committee.

In addition to the after midnight ban, the club was ordered to improve communications between staff in the basement and ground floor and to make sure customers did not carry bottles and glasses into the street.

The pub claimed it had had no complaints from neighbours, the council or courts but at the end of the two-day hearing the committee voted to restrict the licence to midnight from 2am.

Pub manager Brendan Hipwell appealed against the committee's decision at Harrow Magistrates Court on December 19, and the hearing was adjourned to January 17.

Mr Hipwell, who has run the venue for 14 years, said: "I decided to appeal because so many people were asking me when the club was going to re-open."

Ultimately Brendan Hipwell done a good job of persuading the local magistrates and the Sidings was able to have its 2.00am licence restored. Brendan was by now an ever-present at the Railway Hotel having taken back full control, a colourful character he was usually seen with his adopted Teddy Bear who would be wearing a matching waistcoat and telling people 'Teddy doesn't like fighting!' Finally, In August 1996 after fourteen years at the helm of the Railway Hotel, Brendan Hipwell sold the pub to Geoffrey MacIsaac.

THE LEGENDARY BRENDAN HIPWELL PROPRIETOR OF THE RAILWAY HOTEL FOR 14 YEARS

THE END OF THE LINE FOR THE RAILWAY!

With the building now looking very tired and in need of urgent repairs, and of course the ongoing problems with the licence it was not going to be an easy task for Geoffrey MacIsaac. The following year the downstairs hall known for many years as The Sidings was renamed Warrens. Patrick Cronin was to be the man tasked as manager for a large part of this era.

WARRENS NIGHTCLUB
THE RAILWAY HOTEL HARROW

LIVE BAND EVERY SATURDAY
DOORS OPEN 10.00pm - 2.00am
LATE LICENCE

NEW ORIGINALS SATURDAY 31ST MAY
ONE OF LONDONS TOP COVER BANDS

POWER OF SOUL SATURDAY 7th JUNE
SOUL SENSATION

SOUND INJECTION SATURDAY 14th JUNE
NOT TO BE MISSED

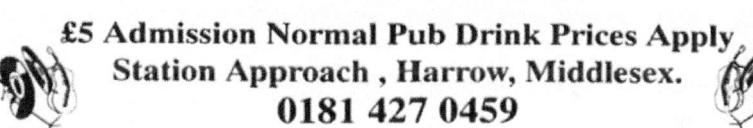

£5 Admission Normal Pub Drink Prices Apply
Station Approach, Harrow, Middlesex.
0181 427 0459

Geoffrey MacIsaac couldn't have asked for a tougher start if he tried, just two weeks in to his new role an existing booking for a wedding turned into a mass brawl which included 70 guests, and gave his new business an unwanted front-page of the local newspaper.

VIOLENCE FLARES IN SUMMER HEAT

FIGHTING wedding guests and rampaging youths were involved in a weekend of booze-filled summer madness at Harrow's pubs.

BY DAVID BROWN

Police admitted they were stretched to the limit as a record level of violence flared across the borough during the mini-heat wave.

Gangs of brawling thugs brought terror to Pinner High Street on Friday night when around 100 people gathered in the street after the pubs closed.

Fights broke out and police took more than an hour to clear the crowd.

On the following night more than 70 wedding guests started a huge brawl at Harrow's most famous music venue, The Railway in Wealdstone.

Police from across north west London were called to deal with the troublemakers and dogs were used to clear the pub and basement club in Railway Approach.

The pub achieved fame in the 1960s as the place where The Who's Pete Townsend first smashed his guitar on stage and rockers Jeff Beck, Jimmy Page and Screaming Lord Sutch launched their careers.

Officers dealt with more than 50 other violent incidents during Saturday night as unconnected violence broke out across Harrow.

Insp Mick Gunnell, who was in charge of policing the borough over the weekend, said: "It was the worst weekend I have had during my time in Harrow.

"We would have been severely stretched if two big incidents had occurred at the same time. As it was we had to call in extra officers from as far away as Harlesden to assist us.

"I have got no idea what caused the trouble – all I can imagine is the hot weather meant people started drinking early in the day and drank more," he added.

Geoffrey MacIsaac, who bought The Railway two weeks ago, said the club had been booked for a wedding reception with 150 guests before he took it over.

He said: "At 10pm I believed it was getting out of control and I called the police to clear the whole place. There was a big fight in the public bar.

"The club is fine, there is no problem with the club. It was not open to the public at the time as it was being used by the wedding guests."

Police arrested five men at the club but they were released without charge because officers felt it was unlikely witnesses would appear in court.

The club's opening hours were restricted to midnight by Harrow Council in October last year after police complained of a "substantial increase in the number of drunken, violent incidents".

But The Railway's then owner, Brendan Hipwell, successfully appealed to Harrow magistrates and its 2am licence was restored.

It must now apply to have the licence renewed in October – but Insp Gunnell said the police would probably not use Saturday's violence as a reason to object to the renewal.

THE PINNER OBSERVER 22ND AUGUST 1996

Despite the ongoing problems that were now starting to taint the name of the Railway Hotel, when the renewal was discussed the new ownership were able to hold onto its late licence. The newly named Warrens Night Club in the basement tried desperately to shake off its now unwanted reputation as a place of trouble, with things slowly but surely returning to some semblance of normality! Successful soul events were held as well as some packed out Rock'N'Roll nights. However, problems were still never far away, and the Police again started to become more and more regular visitors to the Railway. Rumours were abound that the famous old pub and music venue was now very much living on borrowed time!

On Monday 12th October 1998 after 145 years the Railway Hotel's manger, Grainne Hennessy pulled the last pint and shut its doors for the very last time; however the downstairs club, Warrens was to continue to trade at weekends until the end of the month. Early redevelopment ideas that were mooted included amongst others a church!

Rock of ages

Pub where The Who began is poised to become church

BY ROB McNEIL

ROCK band The Who played their first gig there. But now The Railway Hotel is preparing to play host to its biggest star yet — God.

The Station Road venue in Wealdstone has seen its fair share of rock 'n' roll excess over the last 40 years, but planners were last night expected to approve proposals to turn the hotel, now operating as a pub-cum-nightclub, into a church.

"I'm really sad to see it shut," said pub manager Grainne Hennessy as she closed for the last time on Monday. "But, considering the ghosts who are supposed to inhabit the pub, maybe a church would be the best thing to have here."

The pub, used as a morgue after the Wealdstone Rail Disaster in 1952, is reputedly one of Harrow's most haunted buildings, but that didn't stop it becoming a rock 'n' roll venue in the 1960s.

"Mungo Jerry, The Who and Elton John, they all played here," said Grainne, who will be keeping the club part of the Railway operating Fridays to Sundays for the next few weeks. "Even Max Bygraves. This place is a real rock shrine."

It is a pity no one could come forward with the money to refurbish the place, because it has the potential to be a really great venue again.

"I don't know if the church will have planning permission granted, but if they do, good luck to them. They'll have to play great hymns to keep with the tradition of the place."

Another of the musical luminaries of the Sixties who played at the Railway over the years was Harrow's own local lad gone bonkers, Screaming Lord Sutch.

"It was a great venue," he said this week. "There should really be one of those blue plaques on the wall.

"It is a piece of history and it should really be appreciated as such. I hope I have an opportunity to get some of the old lads who played there in its heyday together for a last farewell before they shut it down.

"They should try and get Little Richard to open the church now that he's doing all the evangelical stuff."

THE HARROW OBSERVER DATED 15TH OCTOBER 1998

Upon its closure the building was removed of most of its fixtures and fittings and soon became a target for sustained vandalism, with claims that the building had become unsafe due to, amongst other things its many broken windows. Later, it was claimed that many of these windows had in fact been put through from the inside of what was at the time a locked building, who knows?

What is certainly beyond doubt is that the building was very soon becoming an eyesore and an embarrassment to the council based a few short yards away in the Civic Centre! With the idea of refurbishing the building into a new religion church very soon dropped grand plans were then submitted by London Inns Hotels / Cloisters Care (by now the owners of the building) to build a new ninety nine room hotel over four floors! London Inns was fronted by Duncan Rogers, who had previously been a local councillor. The original plans were submitted in July 1999 before a slightly revised planning application for ninety one bedrooms was considered in November 2000, which was narrowly accepted by the casting vote of the chairman. Concerns were raised that there was insufficient parking for such a hotel, it would appear that plans were later revised to seventy, then fifty five bedrooms.

Bid to build hotel on music pub site

A DERELICT pub which has been boarded up for more than six months could be pulled down to make way for a 55-bedroom hotel.

The proposals for the abandoned Railway Tavern in The Bridge, Wealdstone, include demolishing the building — all the windows of which are already smashed or boarded up — and building a hotel of two, three and four storeys on the slope, with car parking at the back.

The plans will be considered by Harrow councillors, possibly next month.

The applicant, Station Road-based Cloisters Care, which owns the pub, has been in discussions with Harrow Council about the size of the new development for months. During that time the pub has become increasingly vandalised.

The demolition marks the end of an era for a pub — Harrow's biggest music venue in the Sixties — where such groups as The Who and The Rolling Stones appeared in their early days.

A spokesman for Cloisters Care said: "The building has been empty now for about six months. We are already negotiating with a couple of building companies.

"We're unhappy about the way in which the building has been vandalised and are in the process of making it secure after another break-in."

THE HARROW OBSERVER DATED 27TH MAY 1999

With the Railway Hotel deteriorating literally by the day a fire occurred on Monday 8th November 1999, which caused even more damage predominantly to the downstairs function room. The fire was treated as arson, but nobody was ever found or charged. Although burnt and badly vandalised the building was at the time still saveable!

■ **WEALDSTONE:** A boarded-up pub was set alight, causing damage to a downstairs room. Firefighters were called to the Railway Hotel in Railway Approach at 2.20pm on Monday last week by a passer-by who saw the flames. Police are treating the fire as arson. Witnesses should call Det Con Kurt Taylor on 733 3485.

THE HARROW OBSERVER REPORTS THE 'FIRST' FIRE IN ITS 18TH NOVEMBER 1999 EDITION

On Sunday 29th February 2000, Lucy Challis former barmaid at the Railway Hotel received a phone call from her husband to tell her that it was on fire! Lucy relates what she did next 'I went straight up there, and stood watching with tears rolling down my cheeks – the end of an era'. With the Railway Hotel now looking like a very sad looking monument to its former glories a major fire finally put paid to any lingering doubts that the building was saveable. There have been many accusations made that it was an insurance job etc. However, a well-known insurance broker told me that it was probably unlikely. The building would have been insured for a possible rebuild, but permission had already been granted to demolish the building anyway. It would be highly unlikely that any such claim would not have been rigorously examined for a potentially fraudulent act; the majority of these types of claims are never paid out!

What is beyond any doubt is that there was now a lot less building left to demolish, the official report was suspected arson, for which nobody has ever been charged! Incidentally, it was found that most or all of the internal doors in the building were missing, which would make any chance of containing a spreading fire virtually impossible!

Rock shrine goes to blazes

Fire destroys pub which launched The Who

Fire destroys the home of rock legends

BY CHRISTIAN DUFFIN

ONE of Harrow's best-known pubs — once featured on the cover of an album by Sixties stars The Who — has been completely destroyed by fire.

The Railway Hotel in Station Road, Wealdstone, is now little more than a burnt-out shell after firefighters battled for hours to control the blaze on Sunday evening.

Crews from fire stations across London were at the scene until midnight. Firefighters were unable to enter the disused pub because vandalism had made it unsafe.

The boarded-up building had been sprayed with graffiti and had its windows smashed.

Some sections of the building had been empty for years but planners last year approved its demolition and proposals to replace it with a 70-bedroom hotel.

"Basically, the walls are still there but there's no roof anymore," said a Harrow firefighter. "We couldn't go inside because the handrails were missing from the stairs and there were floorboards missing. There were no doors inside so the fire spread quickly."

Firefighters visited the building last year to take a look round. They feared it could be vandalised. "Buildings like that are prime targets," added the firefighter. "Fires don't just start themselves."

Carlo Little, former drummer with the Rolling Stones, played many gigs with his own band at the Railway Hotel. "It's another loss of a landmark rock 'n' roll venue," he said this week.

Legend has it that guitarist Pete Townshend introduced his trademark guitar-smashing at the venue and that the band were discovered there by their future management team.

"We used to go to the Railway all the time," added Carlo. "In its heyday all sorts of bands played there. The first time I met Ronnie Wood was in the Railway."

Firemen at the blazing building — Picture: GARETH

ABOVE THE HARROW TIMES AND HARROW OBSERVER DENOTING THE SAD END TO THE RAILWAY HOTEL

THE SAD SIGHT OF THE LAST REMAINING WALL OF THE RAILWAY HOTEL FOLLOWING ITS DEMOLITION IN 2002

In March 2003 The Acton Housing Association submitted an application for 41 flats, over 4, 5 and 6 floors. The project was to include affordable housing and was never in any real danger of being refused. Although, previously plans were submitted for a hotel firstly in 1999, and then again two years later, this was a much more agreeable proposal for the London Borough of Harrow.

Not only did it meet a defined housing need it was seen as an enhancement to the Railway Approach frontage, and one that did not impinge on the character of the Harrow and Wealdstone station entrance which is a listed building. Overall, it was considered to have a satisfactory impact on the character and appearance of the area. As part of the proposals the famous cut-through between the Railway Hotel and station car-park would disappear for ever as it was deemed to be 'dingy and isolated'. The building works commenced soon after, with the flats opening in September 2004, as a nod to the former sites musical heritage the two blocks were named after two members of The Who. Roger Daltrey and Keith Moon (Pete Townshend and John Entwistle – not considered for some reason!) were honoured with the newly built Daltry House and Moon House respectively. Someone didn't do their homework properly as the lead singers name was spelt incorrectly, with the misspelt signage still remaining to this day! In 2009 the London Borough of Harrow erected a plaque to denote the significant past history of the Railway Hotel, a nice touch by the council, although the four tiny screws and rawlplugs fixing it to a rear wall were never going to stop a determined memorabilia collector, and not surprisingly it was very soon stolen!

THE WHO

This plaque marks the site of the former Railway Hotel, where The Who made rock history by smashing a guitar during the group's shows in 1964

THE PLAQUE DEDICATED TO THE GLORIOUS HISTORY OF THE RAILWAY HOTEL – UNVEILED IN 2009 AND STOLEN SOON AFTER

Although the Railway Hotel is now long gone the unique layout of the site makes it extremely easy to get your bearings, with the famous slope towards Marlborough Hill still remaining, there is even a small mural a few yards away on the bridge towards Wealdstone Town Centre to further remind you of the sites former glories. Stroll just a few more yards and you will reach the Railway Bar at Barretts, with the strong likelihood of bumping into one or more of the Railway's former stalwarts!

RIP THE RAILWAY HOTEL 1853 – 2000 GONE BUT NEVER FORGOTTEN!

MOON HOUSE AND DALTRY HOUSE NOW OCCUPYING THE FORMER SITE OF THE RAILWAY HOTEL

THE MISSPELT SIGN FOR DALTRY HOUSE AND A MURAL DEPICTING THE RAILWAY ON WEALDSTONE BRIDGE

n.b-: many thanks to the various local newspapers for some of the above information which contains information and names etc. ALL of which is in the public domain. It should be remembered that these types of reports tend to focus on the less savoury events in pubs as the better ones don't command as much interest for some reason!

Also please note The Railway Hotel was the pub's first and last name so is generally referred to as this - although it was also known during its history as The Railway Tavern and simply The Railway!

Dates and order of tenants/managers etc are as per recorded evidence and may possibly vary with certain peoples recollections!

THE RAILWAY HOTEL – LANDLORDS/PROPRIETORS TIMELINE

1861 - ????	-	MR.T.COMLEY
???? - 1878	-	JAMES MARLOW
1878 - ????	-	JAMES URIDGE
1880 - ????	-	MR CLARKE
1884 - 1891	-	LEWIS COLE
1891 - 1892	-	J.H.HODGSON
???? - 1895	-	ERNEST OWERS (OWNER)
1892 - 1897	-	GEORGE LANDER
1897 - 1898 OWNER?)	-	MR.WEIGHT(FREEHOLD
1898 - 1899	-	C.T. (THOMAS) ANDREWS
1899 - 1908	-	H.F.COLLYER
1908 – 1919?	-	EMILY COLLYER

	(FROM 1909 THOMAS, FREDERICK, SILVESTER WAS APPOINTED MANAGER)
1918c - 1958c -	HENRY JAMES HULKS/ H.J.HULKS LIMITED
1968 - 1969 -	DUGALD STEAD
1974 - ? -	THOMAS O'NEILL
1975 – 1976 -	JOHN CHARLES (MANAGER)
1976? - 1977? -	TOM & SUE SPOONER (ST.GEORGES TAVERNS)
1979? - 1980? -	THOMAS GALLAGHER (MANAGER)
1980 - ? -	TOM O'FLAHERTY (MANAGER)
1982 - 1996 -	BRENDAN HIPWELL

(DERRY HIPWELL – BROTHER WAS MANAGER FOR LARGE PERIOD OF THIS TIME)

1996 - ???? -	GEOFFREY MACISAAC (PAT CRONIN MANAGER?)
???? - 1998 -	GRAINNE HENNESSY

(PUB/BAR MANAGER AT TIME OF CLOSURE)

THE MUSICAL LEGACY OF THE RAILWAY HOTEL

Many people's memories of the Railway Hotel will be connected with the various musical events that took place there over the years. A legendary venue that will be forever connected with an infamous event involving Pete Townshend in 1963! A visit there by a young Kevin Rowland would inspire him to write a chart topping hit, and the venue would even have a song written about it!

Here are just some of the household and indeed non-household names, and events that graced the famous old function room 'downstairs at the Railway'.

LONG JOHN BALDRY AND THE HOOCHIE COOCHIE MEN

When Cyril Davies died Long John Baldry (so called after his 6'7" frame) took the nucleus of his Allstar Band and created Long John Baldry and the Hoochie Coochie Men. Eight early gigs were played at the Railway Hotel between 31st January and 14th April 1964. The line-up was as follows; Long John Baldry (vocals/guitar), Rod Stewart (vocals/guitar/harp), Cliff Barton (bass/vocals), Geoff Bradford (lead guitar), Johnny Parker (piano/ Hammond organ) and Ernie O'Malley (drums) all of whom had played in the Cyril Davies set-up! Baldry was known to have not been on the greatest of terms with his predecessor even changing the club night to Baldry's Blues Club at the Railway Hotel.

The Hoochie Coochie Men lasted just over a year before streamlining their line-up and renaming themselves, Steampacket. Ultimately, of course Rod Stewart went onto enjoy a massively successful solo career, whilst all the former Hoochie Coochie Men remained busy on various projects. As for Long John Baldry he had a successful solo career and was latterly based in Canada where he died in 2005 at the age of 64 following a severe chest infection. In 1967 Baldry had a UK number 1 and worldwide hit with 'Let the Heartaches Begin', which still gets plenty of airplay to this day!

**LONG JOHN BALDRY AND THE HOOCHIE COOCHIE MEN FEATURING ROD STEWART ON VOCALS
1964**

THE BEACHCOMBERS

The Beachcombers were a local band who were on the same circuit as The Who, and played a few times at the Railway Hotel before them. The proximity of the venue meant that it was also a good place for them to rehearse. In the early part of their career they were very much a covers band, who would perform the hits of the day from the likes of The Shadows and Buddy Holly. In their band was a young sixteen year old drummer from Wembley by the name of Keith Moon, who would return to the Railway Hotel very soon with his new band The Who. Although Moon defected to their local rivals both camps remained good friends, and John Schollar, the bands guitarist has spoken at various conventions about Moonies pre-Who days. A good local band that are always spoken fondly about by those who saw them!

CLIFF BENNETT AND THE REBEL ROUSERS

Cliff Bennett and the Rebel Rousers were a Rhythm and Blues/ Beat group that were formed back in 1957 and went on to work with the legendary Joe Meek. Managed for a while by Brian Epstein, their biggest hit came in 1967 with the Paul McCartney penned 'Got to get you in to my Life' which peaked at number 6 in the UK charts. A first visit to the Railway Hotel was made in July 1959, followed by a few in the early sixties, a very accomplished band and certainly one that never really got the true recognition they deserved! Amongst many former ex- Rebel Rousers was Chas Hodges, who later of course, became a household name in Chas and Dave! Hodges however was not in the band during their visits to the Railway Hotel! That aside, a much underrated outfit that are well worth seeking out!

BO STREET RUNNERS

The Bo Street Runners were a R'N'B band that played many times at the Railway Hotel's Friday night Boom Room club. Commencing a residency in November 1963 the initial gigs were not particularly well supported, but eventually word got around and they were soon packing the place on a Sunday night! Initially they were playing at various Young Communist League events in and around Harrow and Wembley with the picture below showing one of their earliest outings at the Railway Hotel circa 1963.

Formed in Harrow they were initially called the Roadrunners, but changed the name when it became evident that another band was using that name. In 1964 they entered a competition to find the 'next Beatles' earning a recording contract with Decca and a £1000 prize. In 1965 Mick Fleetwood had a brief stint as drummer with the group, before disbanding the following year! Mick Fleetwood, of course went onto form Fleetwood Mac (even playing at the Railway Hotel). Bo Street Runners were a light that shined bright but only very briefly, with their much sought after recordings commanding very good prices. A sadly much forgotten, but a very important part of the legendary R'N'B scene at the Railway Hotel.

BONZO DOG DOO-DAH BAND

The Bonzo Dog Doo-Dah Band was a psychedelic rock band that played the Railway Hotel c1967 and was renowned for their surreal nature of performing. They were led by Vivien Stanshall (a side kick of Keith Moon) and scored a top five hit in 1968 with 'I'm the Urban Spaceman'

MAX BYGRAVES

Max Bygraves attended a wedding with local Bond girl, Shirley Eaton in the late sixties, and almost certainly (surely) treated the party to a rendition of 'You're a Pink Toothbrush'.

SAVOY BROWN

Savoy Brown was another popular blues band that was at the forefront of the British Blues scene and had their early roots at the Railway Hotel. Playing in what was somewhat a boom time for this type of music in 1968, they were very soon to make their mark across the pond in the USA. Another band that has had various gestations over the years the one constant being Kim Simmonds who still plays with them to this day, with the majority of their appearances these days tending to be in America.

A GREAT OLD SNAP FROM THE ERA – AND POSSIBLY TAKEN AT THE RAILWAY HOTEL

THE CAT

The Cat was as Blues band that had a Friday night residency for a few weeks at the Railway Hotel in 1967.

EVERY FRIDAY
the CAT
RAILWAY HOTEL
HARROW & WEALDSTONE
PLUS Barrie James'
Golden Goodies Disc Show!

CHICKEN SHACK

Chicken Shack are a Rhythm and Blues band that were formed in the mid-sixties by Stan Webb, and played a few times at the Railway Hotel, notably on 1st August 1968, when they featured a very pregnant Christine Perfect in their line up. Perfect would ultimately leave the group and marry John McVie of Fleetwood Mac. The band split up for a couple of years in the mid-seventies, before reforming and still continues to this day. However, Stan Webb is the only member to have remained a constant in their line up. Although they would never achieve massive sales on the singles front (the biggest hit being 'I'd Rather go Blind') they have recorded many albums that have gone on to do well.

CHICKEN SHACK PICTURED IN 1968

CRAZY CAVAN

Crazy Cavan played a number of gigs at the Wednesday night Rock'N'Roll club during 1972, and was always popular, playing to large numbers every week. Also known as Crazy Cavan 'n' the Rhythm Rockers and Cavan & the Rhythm Rockers they were a Teddy boy band from South Wales, formed in 1970, and were still touring and recording right up their frontman Cavan Grogan's death in 2020.

FRONTMAN CAVAN GROGAN c 1972

CUDDLES

Cuddles (not to be confused with Keith Harris's Monkey!) real name Roy Osborne was a Rock'N'Roll fanatic and a singer of 'limited' ability. Apparently, he was a well-known attendee at Rock'N'Roll gigs and hailed from St. Albans. One speciality was to invade the stages of performers such as Jerry Lee Lewis at the London Palladium and remove his shirt! A loveable and eccentric character, he was also a volunteer at Radio Northwick Park when not sweeping the streets of his home town. Somehow, Cuddles blagged a gig at the Railway Hotel in late 1972 for what appears to be his one and only performance there!

CYRIL DAVIES & HIS RHYTHM AND BLUES ALLSTARS

Cyril Davies was an unlikely pioneer of the British rhythm and blues movement, whose work was to have an impact on the likes of The Who, Rod Stewart and the Rolling Stones. Born in 1932 in Denham, Bucks, he very soon became obsessed by this type of music. A railway worker during the day but an accomplished blues musician during the night, with his harmonica playing the stuff of legend! Having played at various venues with Long John Baldry acting as singer, a new venture was started in 1962 when he opened the popular R'N'B club on a Tuesday night at the Railway on 11th December.

CYRIL DAVIES
R & B
ALL - STARS

TUESDAY
RAILWAY HOTEL
Harrow, Wealdstone,
7.30 p.m.

An unlikely looking 'wanabee' pop star, his look and appearance was very much at odds with the likes of Baldry and the up and coming Rod Stewart, for Davies it was purely about the music! Having played at the usual 'haunts' of the time such as the Marquee, and Eel Pie Island he was seemingly on a crusade to bring the 'blues to the masses! The Railway Hotel's R'N'B night soon became a thriving entity which went on to create a legacy and a reputation for the finest of its kind in that area of London!

Cyril Davies and his band were, however, at odds many times as some favoured the 'crowd pleasers' and some the more obscure and experimental forms of the Blues! One such member was Long John Baldry, who was seemingly less than enamoured with his leader. Richard Barnes a friend of Pete Townshend and later promoter of his own club at the Railway gives his take on the fraught relationship thus:-

'I remember Baldry absolutely detested Davies, they were poles apart. Davies was this old balding guy (Davies was only in his early thirties) who worked on the railways during the day. Scruffy old trousers and always drunk. One night Cyril had got blind drunk and had fallen down asleep at the side of the stage, and Baldry was kicking him saying 'you old cunt.' I went off Baldry after that but it worked for a little while and seeing Cyril Davies was a turning point for me. He got me interested in R&B and from his audience at the Crawdaddy! Richmond Club, I became aware of Mods.'

Davies contracted pleurisy in 1963, and was to self-medicate with alcohol in an attempt to relieve the constant pain he was in, all the while working during the day and constantly touring. The illness and his attempts to quell it finally caught up with him when he collapsed on stage at a gig at Eel Pie Island in January 1964. Cyril Davies was not to recover and the world lost a true pioneer of the British R'N'B scene at the tragically young age of 31. The scene and indeed the Railway Hotel owe Davies a huge debt of gratitude for what was a brief but immeasurable contribution.

CYRIL DAVIES THE UNLIKELY LOOKING HERO OF BRITISH RHYTHM & BLUES MUSIC IN THE EARLY SIXTIES

CYRIL DAVIES ALL-STARS

BRITAIN'S LEADING R&B GROUP

EVERY WEDNESDAY
★ **PICCADILLY JAZZ CLUB** ★
(Opp. Windmill Theatre)

EVERY THURSDAY
★ **MARQUEE JAZZ CLUB** ★

EVERY FRIDAY
★ **ROARING TWENTIES** ★
(50 Carnaby Street, London, W.1.)

EVERY TUESDAY
★ **RAILWAY HOTEL** ★
(Harrow, Wealdstone)

EALing 1572 • ENQUIRIES • GERrard 6602

THE DELTAS

The Deltas played the Railway Hotel on 16th January 1998, so would have been one of the last bands to have appeared there. A riotous Rockabilly act, that still tours forty years on from their formation in 1980. The following picture shows them on stage (c1980) at the legendary Royalty Ballroom in Southgate, a venue that was used a few years previous as a location for the film, Quadrophenia.

DESMOND DEKKER

Desmond Dekker played the Railway Hotel on 6th December 1970 and was a Jamaican Ska and Reggae singer-songwriter. Performing with his backing group The Aces he arrived on the back of three major hits, "Israelites" (1968) "007 (Shanty Town)" (1967), and "You Can Get It If You Really Want" (1970). A Reggae legend who had been signed to the legendary Island and Trojan labels he was still performing right up to his death of a heart attack in 2006 at the age of sixty four.

DEXYS MIDNIGHT RUNNERS

Back in '68 in a sweaty club

(Oh, Geno)

Before Jimmy's Machine and the Rocksteady Rub

(Oh, Geno)

On a night when flowers didn't suit my shoes

After a week of flunkin' and bunkin' school

The lowest head in the crowd that night

Just practicin' steps and keepin' outta the fights

Most people are aware that Dexys Midnight Runners 1979 number one hit Geno was based upon lead singer, Kevin Rowland's experience of watching soul legend, Geno Washington, but not maybe, so many are aware that this happened at the Railway Hotel! Kevin Rowland lived at the time in Edgware and recalls the gig thus *"I saw Geno Washington in 68 at the Railway Hotel in Harrow. I was 15 years old and out with all the older kids – you had to be 18 to get in – short-haired, cool-looking mods-turning-into-skinhead types. Looking back, it's probably not the best gig I've ever been to, but I didn't have anything to compare it to"*. For the record there is no record of Geno Washington playing at the Railway Hotel in 1968, so it's highly likely that Rowland's visit was actually in 1969! Maybe, he was actually there late in 1968 to witness the performance of Johnny Johnson and the Bandwagon perform Breaking Down the Walls of Heartache – which he subsequently covered for the B-side of Geno!

Kevin Rowland went onto to visit the Railway Hotel on a number of occasions, but no further visits were to give him such great ammunition for a hit song!

DOC. K'S

Originally formed by Ashley Hutchings in 1967, who subsequently went onto join Fairport Convention, Doc K's were early stalwarts of the British Blues and R&B scene. Still touring to this day they have had many members who have gone onto join other groups of that ilk including, Geoff Krivitt (John Mayall's Bluesbreakers) and Eric Peachey (East of Eden and the Mick Taylor Band). Their gig at the Railway Hotel came during the boom time of R&B there in July 1968.

THE AYNSLEY DUNBAR RETALIATION

July 1968 saw the Aynsley Dunbar Retaliation debut at the Railway Hotel. A blues band which was fronted by the drummer of the same name. Dunbar already had a commendable pedigree having played with The Mojos, John Mayall's Bluesbreakers and The Jeff Beck Group. When Dunbar founded The Aynsley Dunbar Retaliation it was so named as retaliation against John Mayall who had sacked him to be replaced by Mick Fleetwood. After four albums the band split, with Dunbar going on to play with the likes of Frank Zappa, Whitesnake and The Animals, a busy and well respected career saw him being inducted into the Rock and Roll Hall of Fame in 2017.

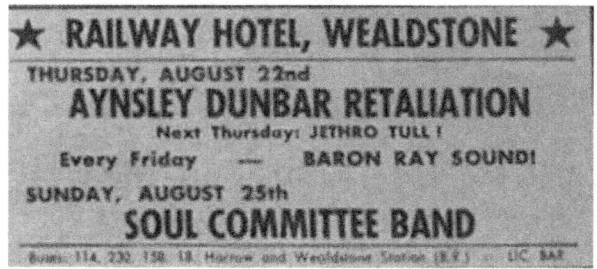

THE EXILED

The Exiled were a Rock'N'Roll band that played the Two R's club at the Railway Hotel in 1966.

THE FANTASTICS

The Fantastics played at the Railway Hotel on 1st November 1970 and had previously been known as The Velours, and had been touring America under that name since the late fifties. A name change came about in 1968, and they developed into more of a vocal group much akin to The Drifters. Hailing from New York they will probably be best remembered for their 1971 hit, Something Old, Something New.

FLASH

Flash were a prog/rock band that played at the Railway Hotel in the early seventies and formed by the former guitarist with Yes, Peter Banks. The band failed to chart in the UK but had a top 30 hit in America with, Small Beginnings.

FLEETWOOD MAC

Fleetwood Mac played the Railway Hotel on Thursday 31st October 1968, having been formed the previous year. Peter Green had left the blues band John Mayall & the Bluesbreakers, and teamed up with Mick Fleetwood to launch a very early version of what would be a globally bestselling outfit who went onto have hits in every corner of the world. Peter Green was to leave early in 1970 having left them with many gems such as 'Albatross', sadly he battled for many years with mental illness and died in July 2020. Fleetwood Mac, of course are still able to sell out the biggest venues all over the world, just like they did that Thursday night at the Railway back in 1968.

THE GREAT HUNGER

The Great Hunger played a few Saturday nights at the Railway Hotel in the early nineties, with the main protagonists being Gerry Brown (see The New Miami Showband) and Steve Travers. Steve Travers was a member of the original Miami Showband and survived the massacre of his fellow band members in 1975. Steve Travers is pictured on extreme right of the picture below, showing his ex-band mates shortly before the tragedy.

THE GREATEST SHOW ON EARTH BAND

The Greatest Show on Earth Band was a British prog/rock band that played the Railway Hotel on 4th August 1968. They went onto record two albums on the EMI label, with their biggest hit coming in 1970 with 'Real Cool World'.

OWEN GREY

Owen Grey (sometimes billed as Owen Gray) performed on a Sunday night in July 1968. A well respected man within Jamaican music his work included, Reggae, R&B, Ska and Rocksteady, and was signed to Island records (his single Patricia in 1960 was their first release) and later the iconic Trojan label. Enjoying the reputation as Jamaica's first home-grown singing star he is now in his eighties, he still performs to this day with his set mainly comprising of ballads and gospel music.

THE HELLRAISERS

The Hellraisers who had previously been known as the Houseshakers were a Rock'N'Roll band who featured Terry Clemson and Graham Fenton, and had previously worked as backing musicians for Gene Vincent on his European tour. Playing at the Railway in 1972, Fenton was to play with various bands before launching a revamped version of Matchbox another Rockabilly outfit that had previously enjoyed chart success with 'I'm a Rockabilly Rebel'. Terry Clemson is still playing with a similar band called the TT's.

THE HEROES

When pub-rock returned to the Railway Hotel in 1975 after a ten year hiatus The Heroes (not to be confused with a band of the same name formed a few years later) were chosen as the opening act. The Hertfordshire based outfit even had a tenuous link to the Railway Hotel's famous ex-residency band, The Who. The guitarist Jack James had previously been in a band with Simon Townshend, brother of Pete and now a member of The Who's touring band.

PUB-ROCK BACK AT THE 'RAILWAY'

TEN YEARS AGO, the pub-rock scene in Harrow was at its peak, the venue being the Railway Hotel in Wealdstone. Bands like The Who figured among the artists who appeared there and went on to become large, if not great names.

On July 29 the Railway is turning back the pages and starting the story again.

The band with the task of making the opening night a success is The Heroes, four lads in their mid-twenties who are far from being newcomers to the music machine.

Jack James, the lead guitarist, was formerly with Clear Peace playing alongside Pete Townshend's Brothers, Simon and Paul.

Bob Clarke, the band's drummer, comes from Virjin, playing mainly on the pub scene, including the late Lord Nelson which has recently become a disco.

Pete Toch, the bassist, and Greg Jeffreys, who plays keyboards, both come from an electric acoustic band called Rosedale Intake. Before that, Greg was studying for a music degree, but he gave it up when the opportunity to enter live rock came his way.

The Heroes were formed about 11 weeks ago by Pete and Greg, and are now under the wing of Mick Cordell, an agent from Watford. It was Cordell who discussed the idea of reopening the Railway with the hotel's manager, John Corriden, and so it began.

The idea is to be an experiment for the first month, when they hope to clear their initial expenditure of £200. They will charge about 20p entrance, though after the first month it will probably be free.

The Heroes, "a rock band with a difference", are hoping to go to Cesar's Palace later on.

BELOW: Riding the rails to re-open the old rock venue at Wealdstone's Railway Hotel are members of the group, The Heros (L/R) Peter Toch, Bob Clarke, Greg Jeffreys and Jack James.

THE HEROES PICTURED OUTSIDE THE RAILWAY HOTEL IN THE HARROW OBSERVER 25TH JULY 1975

THE INTERSTATE ROAD SHOW

A nine piece Beat and Psychedelic group who played at the Railway Hotel in November 1968, they went on to release one single, All I Wanna Do Is Love You/ Grindy, Grind the following year.

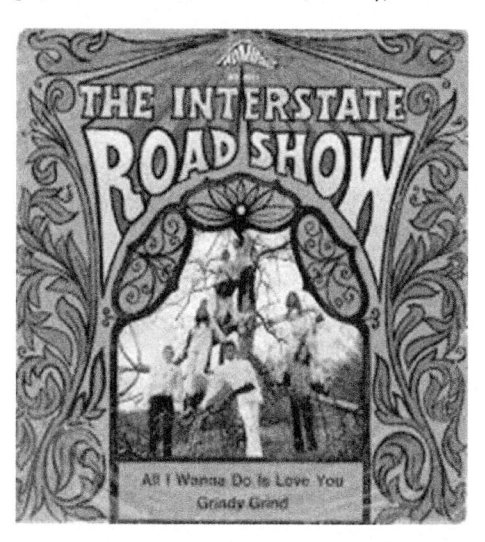

JIMMY JAMES AND THE VAGABONDS

Jimmy James and the Vagabonds is a Soul/Ska outfit that played the Railway Hotel on 6th December 1970. The band was originally formed in the mid-sixties, but in 1970 the original Vagabonds split up, however as Jimmy James owned the name he continues to tour (in his eightieth year) and use it right up to the current day. With to date in excess of fifty band members playing at various times for the Vagabonds, The bands biggest chart success was to come in 1973 with 'I'll Go Where Your Music Takes Me'.

THE LEGENDARY JIMMY JAMES c 1970

JETHRO TULL

11th July and 29th August 1968 (plus an unknown date earlier that year) saw an early incarnation of Jethro Tull play to packed houses at the Railway Hotel. Hailing from Blackpool in Lancashire, Jethro Tull were initially a blues rock/ jazz fusion outfit that went on to add folk, progressive and hard rock to their armoury.

Within a year Jethro Tull had swapped the stage of the Railway Hotel to that of the Royal Albert Hall before eventually playing some of the biggest halls and arenas in the UK. The seventies were arguably the bands golden years, and although many band members have come and gone there is still an incarnation of the band that continues to tour to this day!

JETHRO TULL PICTURED AROUND THE TIME THAT THEY APPEARED AT THE RAILWAY HOTEL

JOE AND BRENDAN

Joe and Brendan were a popular singing duo that played many Sunday Night slots at the Railway Hotel in the early nineties.

ELTON JOHN

Although never appearing at the Railway Hotel as a solo artist, Elton John (then Reg Dwight) is known to have appeared at the Railway Hotel a few times with his band, Bluesology. For a short period they were the backing band for Long John Baldry, and would have appeared c1966. Elton was from nearby Pinner, and is known to have attended a couple of the gigs by The Who, and as it is highly likely that he may have filled in for other bands on the keyboards on an as and when basis! Of course, Elton John has gone on to become one of the biggest selling artists on the planet, and still able in his seventies to sell out massive venues worldwide.

A YOUNG ELTON JOHN WITH MEMBERS OF BLUESOLOGY c1966

JOHNNY JOHNSON AND THE BANDWAGON

Johnny Johnson (whose real name was actually Johnny Mathis, but changed it for obvious reasons) and the Bandwagon played the Railway Hotel on 8th November 1970. Sometimes billed as just the Bandwagon their biggest hit was in 1968 with 'Breaking Down the Walls of Heartache'. Ironically this song was covered by Dexys Midnight Runners on the B-side of 'Geno', so it's more than possible that Kevin Rowland was there that night. Sadly Johnson passed away in 1979 after a long battle with cancer.

BEN E. KING

On Sunday 15th November 1970 the legendary Soul star Ben E. King made a surprise and relatively short noticed visit to the Railway Hotel. In the UK to promote a greatest hits album he played a very small numbers of gigs with the visit to the railway his only one in the capital. Formerly a member of The Drifters, King left them in 1960 to pursue a solo career following various contractual difficulties.

Although King was the singer on many of their songs during his time with them, he was rarely seen on any of their many TV appearances, with a fellow band member lip syncing to his vocals.

In 1961 King scored a worldwide hit with Stand by Me, which was later used to great effect in the 1986 film of the same name. The popular song has been covered by many artists over the years not least of all by John Lennon. King died in 2015 at the age of seventy six of a heart related illness!

> **SUNDAY, NOVEMBER 15th**
> **From U.S.A. — Only London Show**
> **BEN E KING**
> 8-11pm   Please be early!
> Railway Hotel, Wealdstone.
> Harrow and Wealdstone Station (BR and LTE). Buses 114, 158, 182, 286, 186, H1, 140

LEGEND

Legend was a Rock/Blues band that were formed in 1968 by Mickey Jupp, and played the Railway Hotel on 4th June 1970, but split very soon after. Mickey Jupp then went onto be a staple of the Essex pub-rock scene.

CARLO LITTLE

Carlo Little was a legendary local drummer who was in an early incarnation of the Rolling Stones and hailed from Wembley, a pretty good breeding ground for stick men. Wembley was also the home of Charlie Watts, Ginger Baker and Keith Moon, with the later approaching Carlo for drumming lessons before he turned professional. Initially Carlo joined Screaming Lord Sutch and the Savages, before moving on to Cyril Davies All Stars, then the Rolling Stones. Brian Jones who was very much the leader of the Rolling Stones at the time was known to be keen on Carlo joining the band full time, but eventually that honour, of course went to his fellow townsman, Charlie Watts in 1963.

Throughout the sixties Carlo Little was a much sought after session musician, playing on various albums and tours throughout Europe. A top musician who graced the stage of the Railway Hotel on many occasions with various bands, he was also involved in promoting and helping to organise various events there over the years, and will forever have his name linked with the venue! . Sadly Carlo died in August 2005 of lung cancer in Tyne& Wear, where he had lived for a few years!

THE LEGENDARY CARLO LITTLE A MASSIVE PART OF THE HISTORY AT THE RAILWAY HOTEL

THE MOPEDS with CYNDY STAR

Originally billed as The Mopeds with Cyndy Star this sixties Reggae outfit played the Railway Hotel on Sunday 21st July 1968, before renaming themselves Cyndy Star and the Mopeds. There was to be just one single release the same year, The Way I Do/Sad Movie on the Columbia Blue Beat label, which now fetches in excess of £30 on auction websites. Quite what ever happened to Cyndy Star and the Mopeds is a bit of a mystery, with many bands subsequently going on to use similar names!

THE NEW MIAMI SHOWBAND

In 1996, Gerry Brown brother of the Irish Eurovision star Dana resurrected The Miami Showband, with one of their first gigs coming at the Railway Hotel. The original Miami Showband were a massive outfit who sold out venues all over Ireland before the notorious incident in 1975 when they were ambushed on their way back from a gig and three members were shot dead. Gerry Brown's version had very tenuous links to the original band, although they covered all of their hits, and it appears this version was a short lived project before members of the original band relaunched a few years later.

DANA AND HER BROTHER GERRY BROWN

THE NEW ORIGINALS

The New Originals are a cover band who played downstairs at the Railway Hotel on 31st May 1997. The band is still in existence to this day and plays the likes of Weddings and Holiday Camps.

FREDDIE NOTES AND THE RUDIES

Freddie Notes and The Rudies played the Railway Hotel on 18th October 1970, and were a British reggae band that very soon after changed their name to The Greyhounds. In 1971 the newly named band scored a massive hit with, Black and White, a song which was to be covered by numerous artists over the years. Freddie Notes still performs predominantly at Ska and Reggae festivals.

FREDDIE NOTES AND THE RUDIES c1970

THE PIONEERS

The Pioneers played at the Railway Hotel on 25th October 1970 and were a Reggae trio that went through various line-up changes, but at the time of their visit to Wealdstone comprised of brothers Derrick and Sydney Crooks, and George Aggard (half-brother of Desmond Dekker). The bands most famous recording was 'Longshot Kick the Bucket' on the Trojan Label in 1969, having released an incredible thirteen singles the previous year! The group are still active and touring to this day, having gone through various changes of personnel.

POWER OF SOUL

Ruislip based soul band that were formed in 1986 and still very active around the West London area, they are predominantly a covers band with a great reputation. Having been forced to end a long time residency at the Plough in Kenton due to the brewers converting the performance area to an eatery, they relocated for a short while to the Railway Hotel in March 1991.

THE PUNK ROCK CONNECTION

The Railway Hotel can't claim to be at the forefront of the Punk Rock revolution that was emerging during 1976/7 in terms of a venue for the upcoming bands of the day, there were, however, known to be local bands of that ilk that made use of the rehearsal facilities.

However, one of the most important meetings in the gestation of Punk did occur there during the sixties. Vivienne Westwood who had trained at nearby Harrow Arts School was at the time married to Derek Westwood who as well as being employed in a local Hoover factory run a weekly rock and roll club at the Railway. Fate was to intervene at one of these nights when a slightly younger Malcolm McLaren attended, and before long he and Vivienne were an item!

Moving swiftly out of the area the couple went onto launch various business ventures including a clothes shop in Chelsea named SEX. This venue became a magnet to the individuals who wanted to break from the norm, and was where McLaren first met a young John Lydon (later to become Johnny Rotten). McLaren masterminded the birth of his new band called The Sex Pistols, a band that was to change everything – nothing in Music would ever be the same again!

How different things may have been for the UK music scene if McLaren and Westwood had not met that fateful day at the Railway some years before!

THE PYRAMIDS

A British Ska and Reggae band that played the Railway Hotel on 13th December 1970, they had actually changed their name to Symarip probably due to the fact that at the time another band playing Surf music was using that name! Their biggest and most well-known hit was Skinhead Moonstomp, a track that went onto be covered by countless Ska bands over the years, Symarip still perform, albeit on a fairly infrequent basis!

THE PYRAMIDS c 1970

JOHNNY QUANTRELL AND THE CONFEDERATES

If there was one person who loved every minute of his many gigs at the Railway Hotel it was Johnny Quantrell (real name – Ian Charlesworth), so much so that he wrote a song 'Rocking at the Railway Hotel' which is available to watch on youtube.

A local band from Harrow, in 1975 Johnny Quantrell and the Confederates appeared on the ITV talent show, Opportunity Knocks which was watched by in excess of 18million viewers! Peter Moss who played guitar also had some success as a playwright, penning one which went on to star Anna Karen (Olive from On the Buses) in a small theatre in London.

Johnny Quantrell and the Confederates played pure Rock and Roll and toured the length and breadth of the country, with the occasional foray abroad. Although predominately covering other bands Rockabilly numbers they would also perform their own stuff, some of which made it on to cd releases.

A PHOTOGRAPH FROM LATE IN THE BANDS CAREER– JOHNNY QUANTRELL SEATED CONTINUED TO BRAVELY PERFORM RIGHT THROUGHOUT HIS ILLNESS

Ian Charlesworth sadly passed away after a long and courageous battle with cancer on Saturday 2nd March 2019.

Opportunity Knocks for Harrow based pop group "Johnny Quantrell and the Confederates" when they appear on television on Easter Monday. The band is (left to right): Johnny Quantrell, Stuart Colman, Peter Moss and Mac Poole.

RACING CARS

Racing Cars were a Welsh Pop/Rock band who played at the Railway Hotel sometime in 1976 having just signed for Chrysalis Records. The night they played at the Railway they performed their new single 'They Shoot Horses Don't They?' which was homage to the film of the same name. Racing Cars scored a big hit that was to remain in the charts for weeks! 'They Shoot Horses Don't They?' was to be their one and only chart hit, and within a couple of years they had split up.

THE ROLLING STONES

There are people who will swear to have seen the Rolling Stones perform at the Railway Hotel, sadly they didn't, although their drummer from an early incarnation Carlo Little did many times! People who say they saw the Stones at the Railway may well be getting confused with the time that they supported The Ronnetts in January 1964 at the nearby Granada cinema.

THE SEAGUEL AND ROD FELLAS TRIO

The Seaguel and Rod Fellas Trio was a Folk/Irish outfit that had a weekend residency at the Railway Hotel during 1975.

MUSIC
SATURDAYS AND SUNDAYS
THE SEAGUEL AND
ROD FOLLAS TRIO
RAILWAY HOTEL
WEALDSTONE
Next to Station
427 0459
S06224

SHAKIN' STEVENS AND THE SUNSETS

There was a packed house to see a pre-solo Shakin' Stevens at the weekly Rock'N'Roll in early May of 1972, billed as the groups only London appearance! Although, not yet the major star he was to become in the eighties, Shakin' Stevens and the Sunsets were a busy and very popular touring band who had released a few albums with moderate success. However, when Stevens (real name, Michael Barratt) was spotted by Jack Good he was deemed to be perfect for the lead role in his new West End show – Elvis!

The success of the show and the ultimate clamour for 'Shaky' as he had by this time been dubbed meant that the days of touring with The Sunsets were gone for good. Following the success in the Theatre, Stevens released 'This Ole House' which was a massive hit ending up as his first number 1. Hit after hit were to follow totalling 33 in the top forty, earning him the title of top-selling singles artist of the eighties! As for The Sunsets they still tour to this day, albeit with a much changed line-up!

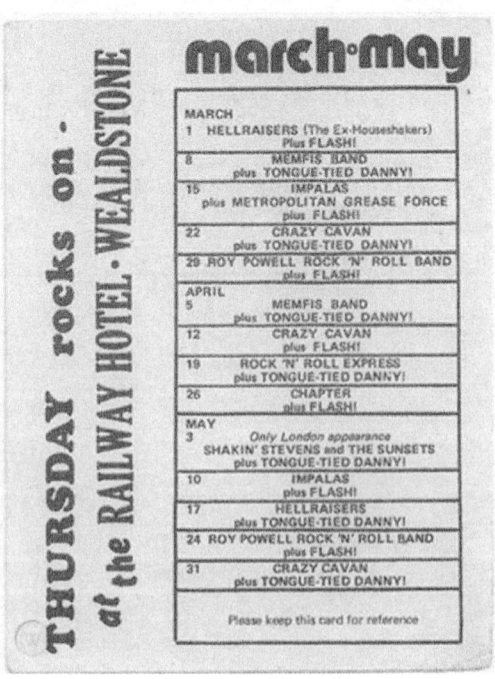

MEMBERSHIP CARD FOR THE THURSDAY ROCK AND ROLL CLUB – 1972

THE SISTER ACT THEATRE COMPANY

The now defunct theatre company performed a female only cabaret about Domestic abuse and violence in June 1989.

THE SKATALITES

The Skatalites were a Reggae/Ska band that played a couple of times at the Railway during the early seventies. Hailing from Jamaica they formed in 1964 and went through various break-ups then reformations, a diluted version of them still tours to this day.

THE SKYWAY 5

The Skyway 5 was a South Harrow based jazz band that appeared on Friday 4th July 1959 during the interval of The Rebel Rousers set. Having been active for less than a month they were given a tiny slot, however the Harrow Observer reported 'that there music was so hot they were retained for a portion of the second half'.

SOMETHING ELSE

Something Else were a Rock'N'Roll band that played a couple of times at the Railway Hotel in 1969. The following is a report from the Harrow Observer in which the reporter seems more interested in one of the group's girlfriends than the actual band itself!

Presents group's image

NOT MANY rock and roll groups can boast a publicity manager as pretty as 19-year-old Lesley White, of 12, Merton Road, Harrow. Her group is called "Something Else," and consists of three talented players who first got together and played at the Railway Hotel, Wealdstone. Their sounds blended well and they agreed to keep together.

Lesley is their biggest fan; her boy friend, Steve Day, is the group's drummer. Lead guitarist is Geoff Runacre and the bass guitarist is "Mitch" Mitchell. Lesley believes in them.

"They're very good. I want to see

Lesley White, Publicity Manager to local "group". See "Presents group's image"

them get to the top. They are talented musicians; only six months together and they have attained considerable fame among rock and roll addicts," she says.

In her working life, Lesley is a secretary to a public relations firm in the West End.

HORATIO SOUL AND THE SQUAREDEALS

Horatio Soul and the Squaredeals was a soul/reggae band that played at the Railway Hotel on 11th August 1968 and was fronted by Hubert Pattison, sometimes performing under his real name and also his other alias, Shubert.

ROD STEWART

Rod Stewart (now Sir Rod Stewart) played five dates at the Railway Hotel from 2nd February to 14th April 1964 as part of Long John Baldry and the Hoochie Coochie Men. Known at the time as 'Rod the Mod' his soulful/bluesy voice was a perfect foil for the Hoochie Coochie Men who had a reputation as a great R&B band. Rod Stewart, of course went onto be a worldwide star with countless Number One's all over the world including the likes of Maggie May and Sailing. Now aged 75 Rod Stewart is still able to sell out stadiums in both the UK and America.

ROD STEWART FROM AROUND THE TIME HE PLAYED AT THE RAILWAY HOTEL

THE FULSON STILLWELL BAND

The Fulson Stillwell band, formed in 1966, were an Ealing based Jazz outfit that played the Railway Hotel on new-year's eve 1967. Infrequent reunions have happened over the years and are not ruled out in the future!

THE FULSON STILLWELL BAND c 1967

SCREAMING LORD SUTCH

Screaming Lord Sutch (real name David Sutch) who lived for many years in South Harrow loved the Railway Hotel, and the Railway Hotel loved him! Many appearances were made, none of which were forgotten by anybody who attended! There are countless examples of Sutch talking fondly about the Railway Hotel, a venue that he had no qualms about comparing with the famous Cavern in Liverpool! A man who had time for everybody that met him he even gave long time barmaid, Lucy Challis a tip of £1M, sadly for Lucy the homemade note featuring Lord Sutch's image as appose to that of the Queen was worthless!

In 1970 (Guy Fawkes Night to be precise) Screaming Lord Sutch and the Savages played, what was billed as their last gig before – David Sutch was to go solo, and go off to tour the States. Although the career without the Savages and his Lordship tag was to be a short-lived affair, a packed house were treated to one of his best ever shows, rounded off by the symbolic burning of an effigy of Englebert Humperdinck (Ted Heath would also have the dubious honour bestowed upon him in the very near future) to herald his claim for total domination of the USA! The report below in the following weeks Harrow Observer details this momentous occasion.

One last scream from Lord Sutch

Remember, remember the fifth of November, gunpowder, treason and Sutch.

That describes the colourful Rock 'n Roll performance of Screaming Lord Sutch at the Railway Rock House last Thursday.

Lord Sutch took to the stage wearing a canary yellow draped jacket with emerald green cuffs and the regulation flowery trousers and, as can be seen from the picture right, put some real heart into the oldies — including "Jack The Ripper" during which he waved a large knife at members of the audience.

Lord Sutch's original backing group The Savages were gathered together specially for the performance at the Railway Hotel, which is the last before he drops the "Screaming" image and heads for a tour of the United States.

The picture below shows Dave Sutch taking on the new cool look that he hopes will flutter the hearts of the female population of America.

Dare it be said that Lord Sutch is moving with the times?

The 400 or so people who went to the Railway Rock House on Thursday will at least remember one of the best performances Screaming Lord Sutch has ever given.

When the time came for the Rock House to close, his lordship screamed his way out into the car park at the rear of the building where a bonfire was waiting to consume an effigy of Englebert Humperdinck — symbolising Sutch's forthcoming challenge to the world of male ballad singers.

Pictures by Ron Reid.

Sutch could always be relied upon to maximise any opportunity of free publicity as detailed in the following when he recalled bygone days at the Railway Hotel. Screaming Lord Sutch had just made a triumphant return to his old haunt as part of the Harrow Arts Festival in 1994. It is interesting see mention of past visitors to the Railway Hotel, including, The Small Faces and The Kinks, neither of whom actually played there! For further reading on this larger than life character you could do worse than get yourself a copy of the brilliant biography by Graham Sharpe entitled ' The Man Who Was Lord Sutch' published in 2005 by Aurum Press. Graham knew Lord Sutch for many years, right up to his tragic death and as young reporter for the local press was the first person phoned when his house was on fire, Sutch informed Graham that he would wait to telephone the Fire Brigade until he got there with a photographer!

Thursday, October 6, 1994 — Observer News and Advertising 081-427 4404 — 77

Leisure

INCLUDING WEEKEND TV GUIDE AND FULL WHAT'S ON LISTINGS

Sixties survivor who just keeps on rocking

IN THE hearts of the teenagers who made the Sixties swing, the water will always drip from the walls of the Railway Hotel.

The Wealdstone pub is one of the few surviving Sixties venues. Liverpool's Cavern is now a car park and London's Marquee has moved, but The Railway remains.

Screaming Lord Sutch and his group The Savages were regular stars on stage at the pub in Railway Approach. Other artists who played there included The Who, Long John Baldry, Rod Stewart, The Small Faces, The Kinks and Elton John.

Still rocking after all these years. Screaming Lord Sutch at The Railway, right.
Picture: EDMOND TERAKOPIAN

The Who paid tribute to the venue for their first gig by picturing The Railway in the centrefold of one of their albums.

Now Sutch and the pub hope to recognise The Railway's contribution to rock 'n' roll with a commemorative plaque and display of memorabilia.

And on Tuesday of last week Sutch returned to the pub as part of Harrow Arts Festival.

"Adults used to hate the strange-looking teenagers who went to The Railway but it really was the place to be if you were young," he recalled.

Rock 'n' roll gigs were banned by many local authorities so The Railway became a mecca for teenagers throughout North-west London.

Entry to gigs cost just two

BY DAVID BROWN

shillings; there was outrage from teenagers when the pub increased charges to half a crown – equivalent to less than 13p today.

"The place would get so crowded that the walls would be dripping with condensation but there was a great atmosphere," said Sutch.

His coffin, cage and bath act at The Railway made him a national celebrity but some of his more bizarre routines led to trouble.

"During my Great Balls of Fire act the curtains caught on fire and the pub had to call the fire brigade. I don't think I got paid," he said.

Groups appearing at the pub in the Sixties were paid £20 a show –

a huge amount considering the average weekly wage was just £15.

"They were great days but they have gone now. Synthesizers are stopping proper musicians getting into the charts now," said Sutch.

The Railway's manager Brendan Hipwell hopes to organise an exhibition of memorabilia – including posters, ticket stubs and photographs – to celebrate the pub's distinguished musical history.

"We regularly get people coming to the pub who went to gigs here in the Sixties and ask to have a look around," said Mr Hipwell.

Conversion of the pub into a disco in the 1970s saw most of the original features destroyed but it now has live music most evenings.

On the 8th November 1997 Screaming Lord Sutch and the Savages rather fittingly ended their time together at the Railway Hotel. On stage that night to join Sutch were Wyatt Wendelt (Drums), Harvey Ellison (Saxophone), long time Savage, Tony Dangerfield (Bass) and Peter Green (Guitar) who having previously worked with the likes of Suzi Quatro has also carved out a career as a record producer and composer.

Just twelve days later Lord Sutch contested his last election for the Monster Raving Loony Party, his forty second in all. This time Sutch contested a seat for a local election in Winchester where he was to receive just over 300 votes which was about his average!

Sadly David Sutch had suffered with depression for many years and on the 16th June 1999 he took his own life at his home in South Harrow. A character that will be forever associated with the Railway Hotel (playing the venue in every decade from the sixties until its closure in the late nineties) its probably quite fitting that he was not around to witness the final sad demise of his beloved venue, but no doubt if he could have chosen to end his career anywhere it would have been there!

Following David Sutch's death the Savages continued without him right up until 2006, but were allegedly a shadow of the former fun and madcap act that they had once been!

THE MUCH MISSED SCREAMING LORD SUTCH - 3RD EARL OF HARROW

TASTE

Taste was an Irish blues and rock band that had been formed by the soon to be legendary songwriter and guitarist, Rory Gallagher in 1966. At least three performances were made at the Railway Hotel in 1968, these being 24th September, 24th October and 31st October 1968. Hailing from Cork, Taste had recently relocated to London, and soon became a stable on the local Rhythm and Blues circuit, with Rory Gallagher's brother, Donal acting as their manager. In 1970 the band played at the legendary Isle of Wight festival which featured amongst others, The Who and Jimmy Hendrix just a few weeks before his death.

Not long after the Isle of Wight festival Taste split up due to various internal matters that had been boiling away for some time. Rory Gallagher went onto have a successful career as a solo artist, and was even courted by The Rolling Stones at one stage; however, he was reportedly happier to plough his own furrow. For many years Gallagher faced a battle with alcoholism, which saw him suffer a failed liver, resulting in over three months in intensive career before losing his fight in June 1995 at just 47 years of age. The following year the other two original members of Taste, Richard McCracken and John Wilson reformed and still perform to this day.

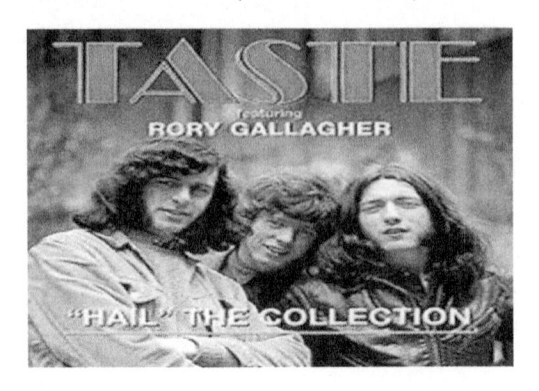

THE T-BONES

Played at the Railway Hotel on 1st September 1964, having been formed the previous year by Gary Farr, they played R&B covers around the local circuit. This gig was as a late replacement for The Who during their twelve week residency there.   The following year they were rebranded as Gary Farr and the T-Bones, as there was an American band of the same name at the time!   Commercial success was to elude them and eventually Gary Farr pursued a solo career   but was to end up as a carpenter in the USA.   Somewhat of a health fanatic Farr lost his life in 1994 at just 49, following a strenuous cycle ride that bought on a heart attack!

TEN YEARS AFTER

Ten Years After played the Railway Hotel on 15th August 1968, and already had two albums in the can, going on to release another seven before they split up in 1974. A blues rock outfit they went on to play the1970 Isle of Wight festival alongside the likes of The Who and Jimmi Hendrix. After a brief comeback in the early eighties they finally reformed in 1988, and still tour to this day with Chick Churchill and Ric Lee.

JOE TEX

Joe Tex was a soul singer who would spend a great deal of his career having to contend with being constantly compared to James Brown. Joe Tex made an appearance at the Railway Hotel on 19th January 1969 having already released in excess of twenty singles in America. The only chart success in the UK came in 1976 with "Ain't Gonna Bump No More (With No Big Fat Woman)", which peaked at number 2. Tex converted to Islam in the mid-sixties and toured under his new name of Yusuf Hazziez preaching the word of Allah. In 1982 he was found near to death at the bottom of his swimming pool, and sadly just five days later died of a massive heart attack at just 47 years of age!

NICKY THOMAS

Nicky Thomas played the Railway hotel on 22nd November 1970 and was riding high on the success of his hit single, Love of the Common People, which was later, covered by Paul Young and resulted in another chart success. A reggae artist he was another stalwart of the legendary Trojan label. He sadly died at the age of forty one in 1990, although never confirmed it is believed he committed suicide.

NICKY THOMAS PICTURED IN 1970

TONGUE-TIED TONY

Tongue-Tied Tony was a well-known Rock'N'Roll DJ who spun his records at the Railway Hotel and many other venues during the 60's and 70's.

THE TOWER OF SOUL

The Tower of Soul (not to be confused by The Power of Soul – who also played the Railway Hotel) was a soul band that played the Railway Hotel on Friday 5th December 1997.

LIVE BAND
TOWER OF SOUL
are at
THE RAILWAY HOTEL
Railway Approach, Harrow
5th December, doors open 10.00pm
DJ WICKED RICKY FROM HELL
50's, 60's, 70's Grooves

GENO WASHINGTON AND THE RAM JAM BAND

Geno Washington played the Railway Hotel on 23rd March 1969, and one can only imagine how good he must have been, a young Kevin Rowland certainly can! Having seen him recently in Norwich at the age of 75, and still on top of his game it must have been a special night!

Geno Washington and the Ram Jam Band were never going to be a prolific recording outfit as they were seemingly never off the road bringing Soul and R and B to the masses, but have released the occasional single and album, with 'Hi Hi Hazel' probably there best known song. A little known fact is that they were originally planned to play as the house band in the 1979 film, Quadrophenia. Geno Washington still tours and is still definitely worth watching!

BELOW A RECENT PICTURE OF THE LEGENDARY GENO WASHINGTON STILL TOURING!

WHATS NEXT

What's Next were a soft rock and covers band that were very popular with the clientele at the Railway Hotel and played regularly there on Friday nights in the late eighties and early nineties.

THE WILD ANGELS

The Wild Angels are a British Rock'N'Roll band who played the Railway Hotel in May 1970, and are still touring today. The band took their name from the 1966 Peter Fonda film of the same name and during the late sixties/early seventies they released nine singles mainly Rock'N'Roll covers.

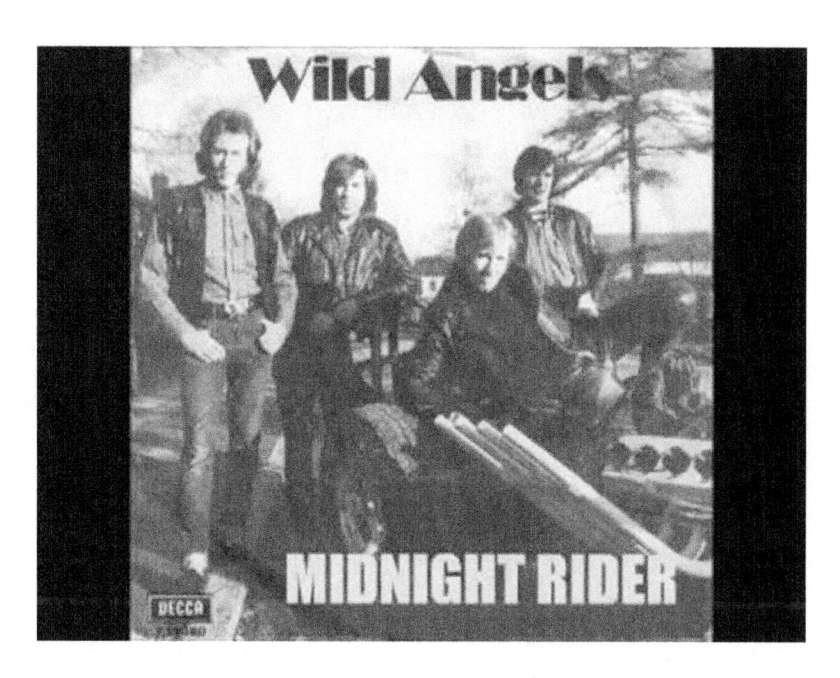

WILD WALLY'S ROCK'N'ROLL SHOW

In 1970, fresh from the release of their Album - Wild Wally's Rock'N'Roll show played the Railway Hotel. Billed as a novelty Rock'N'Roll show they were basically a covers band who's musicianship was said to be pretty good, led by Wild Wally (real name Pete Saunders) they injected comedy into their routine, something that their front man says wasn't captured on vinyl.

WORD 4 WORD

Word 4 Word was a Rock Band that played the Railway Hotel on Thursday 19th August 1993. A local band with some members from the Pinner area, two of their numbers are pictured below with legendary hell raiser Oliver Reed at a previous function.

Rockers Larry Broderick and Phil Donovan with Oliver Reed

THE YARDBIRDS

On Sunday 22nd September 1963 The Yardbirds played their last gig at the Railway Hotel; although they would go on to play a number of dates the following year at the nearby Churchill Hall in Kenton. Originally formed in 1963 as the Metropolitan Blues Quartet they hailed from Surrey and played regularly at the Crawdaddy club in Richmond after the Rolling Stones had finished a residency there. The gig at the Railway Hotel was one of their first under their new name, although it would not have featured Eric Clapton as he didn't join until the following month having replaced Top Topham!

Other members that would have been present that night were Keith Relf (vocals), Chris Dreja (rhythm guitar), Paul Samwell-Smith (bass) and Jim McCarty (drums). The later still tours with a much diluted version of The Yardbirds, almost exclusively in the USA.

JOHN E. YOUNG AND THE TONICKS

A soul band that played the Railway hotel on 18th August 1968 (having played there sometime the previous year), and were for a while (rather confusingly) fronted by Colin Young who left to join The Foundations who went on to have a number 1 hit with, Baby Now That I Found You. The confusion was compounded somewhat as they were also sometimes billed as Joe E.Young and the Tonicks or even Joey Young and the Tonicks. The Tonicks reformed minus Colin Young, but it would appear that this was only for a brief period!

CLUB NIGHTS etc

THE TWO R's CLUB

The Two R's was an early Rock'N'Roll/Jive club that operated at the Railway Club in the late fifties, and run right up to c1967! Around the same time over in East London there was a club with a similar name, the Double R club which was run by the notorious Kray Twins and tended to attract a slightly different clientele!

The first newspaper article comes from the Harrow Observer in 1958 and details a Skifflers competition.

SKIFFLERS' CONTEST

Cy Grant, the television singer, was unable to judge the finals of a skiffle competition organized by the Two R.R.'s Club at the Railway Hotel, Wealdstone, on Monday, because of a last minute television engagement and recording session.

However the competition for which 14 group entered originally, was not delayed and the J. Weeler Group, from Edgware won the £20 prize. Other groups taking part were the Bohemians from Wealdstone, the Zodiacs from Kingsbury, the Skiffle Cats from Willesden, the Sinners from Chelmsford and the Hawks from Peckham.

The judges were Mr. Gallacher and Mr. J. Teirney. Mr. D. J. McCallion was M.C.

TWO R's CLUB
Railway Hotel, Wealdstone

GRAND JIVING CONTEST

FRIDAY, 30th MAY 1958

£10 CASH PRIZE
JIVING SHIELD

8 - 11 p.m.   ADMISSION 2/-
LICENSED BAR

Entries to B. J. McCALLINN
138 RICKMANSWORTH ROAD
PINNER, MIDDX.
or at door on night

TWO R's CLUB
Railway Hotel, Wealdstone

ANNIVERSARY PARTY

MONDAY, 2nd JUNE
8 - 11.30 p.m.

FREE BUFFET   LICENSED BAR
GUEST ARTISTES   JIVING EXHIBITION
MEMBERS TICKETS 5/-

JIVING TO THE JOHNNIE REBS
Please bring your Membership Cards

Two Rs Club
RAILWAY HOTEL WEALDSTONE

NOW OPEN

GRAND JACK-POT PRIZE
£20.0.0 TO BE WON

Jiving to the **JOHNNIE REBS**
EVERY WEEK 8-11
LICENSED BAR   —   ADMISSION 3/6

EVERY FRIDAY
Jiving to the Latest Records 8-11
ADMISSION 2/-   —   LICENSED BAR

SPOT PRIZE **£5.0.0** Every Week

NEW MEMBERSHIP STARTS 1st SEPT.
Buses, Trains to Wealdstone Station

THE TWO R.'s
WITH THE
SYN or PLUM-NELLIE
AT THE RAILWAY HOTEL
WEALDSTONE BRIDGE

FRIDAY, 21st JANUARY & EVERY FRIDAY 8 to 11 p.m.
Buses 158, 114 & 18 pass the door.   Fully Licensed Bar

THE BOTTOM ADVERT FOR THE TWO R's CLUB WAS FROM 1966

STUDIO ONE JAZZ CLUB

In 1959 with Trad Jazz and Jive music very much the order of the day two local friends expanded their thriving Club, which was held in Iver, Bucks, to include a weekly date at the Railway Hotel. The report below from the Harrow Observer in July 1959 states that it's a friendly club for beat hungry teenagers!

New Jazz Club is 'Friendly'

Over 200 "beat-hungry" teenagers went to the Railway Hotel, Wealdstone, last week for over three hours of non-stop jiving and jazz on the first evening of the Studio One Jazz Club.

It has been formed by Mr. Edward Norman, of Ruislip, and Mr. George Drummond, of Uxbridge. They already run a club at Iver.

The club is run on a "friendly basis." All the people who attended were given free membership cards. There were two bands — the "Rebel Rousers" and the "Skyway Five." The latter has only been going for four weeks and the majority of its members live in South Harrow.

THE RAILWAY SOUL CLUB

In 1967 the Railway Soul Club came into being, it would cost you 7s 6d per year membership, and entitled members to a Friday night Disco, and a live performance on a Sunday. As you will see from the following local newspaper report from January 1969 it was a venue that was to have a growing reputation for trouble, something the organisers said was a somewhat harsh summary!

Railway Soul Club

TWO HUNDRED young people every Friday and Sunday night dance to the latest soul sounds socking it to them at a mind-blasting 120 watts at the Railway Hotel, Wealdstone. Says manager and disc-jockey Ray Peterson: "We have been told by the bands that play here that we are one of the top three soul clubs in London for audience response and records played."

The club started over four years ago when the Who played there as the High Numbers, and has been in its present form for over two years. Peterson, who has worked at the Marquee, the Flamingo, the 100 Club, and in Pirate Radio, returned to the place where he started at £3 a night to set up the soul club, "partly because I like soul, partly because it gets the response."

The mixture of discotheque nights on Fridays and live groups on Sundays has secured a growing membership of over 1,000, at 7s 6d per year for new members and 5s for renewals.

The club has received some unfavourable publicity recently. Comments Ray: "It's been over-magnified. We have had six small fights in 18 months and have never called the police in; we have four professional 'stewards' who know their business. I have complete confidence in them.

"In fact, the police have only been in twice. Once they just walked in and out, and the other time they carried out a full offensive weapons raid, including me, and found nothing. We have good relations with the police; they have complimented us on the way we run the club.

"This is not a roughhouse; we run a decent scene."

Future Plans

Plans for the future include expansion to accommodate top American artistes. For example, on Sunday, Joe Tex is making one of his four British appearances at the club. Peterson hopes that things will develop from there.

The council is shortly to build an old people's home nearby. "We shall soundproof the club completely," says Ray. "We don't want to cause any inconvenience."

THE ABOVE FLYER FROM 1968 ALSO DETAILS THE THURSDAY BLUES CLUB

REGGAE AND SOUL CLUB (1970)

On the 18th October the Railway Hotel hosted a regular Reggae and Soul Club every Sunday night. During the clubs short life it managed to entice quite a few big names such as Ben E.King.

ROCK AND ROLL NIGHTS (1969)

A Rock'N'Roll club was started in 1969 it continued to run for a few years every Thursday and Saturday evening. See the flyer from 1972 in the previous Shaking Stevens section.

Rock

Thursday rock 'n roll nights at the Railway Hotel, Wealdstone, have been going for about a year and on Saturday Johnny Quantrell ran his second Saturday night, with his group "Johnny Quantrell and the Confederates".

The line-up of the Confederates is: Adrian Collins (drums), 12, D'Arcy Gardens, Kenton; Steve Papworth (rhythm), 28, Element Close, Pinner; Roger Cooper (bass), 2, Derwent Avenue, Hatch End; and Steve Knibb (lead guitar), 61, Oakfield Avenue, Kenton.

Johnny would put his group in "The Rockhouse" as a resident group but they have been booked for clubs, dances and the University circuit.

The routine at the Railway is group, discs, group; and both are very good. Groups include The Legend (on Saturay May 2), who were on Disco 2 on Saturday night, Good Earth, Wild Wally's Rock n Roll Show, Shakin Stevens and the Sunsets, The Wild Angels, and Screaming Lord Sutch and his Heavy Friends.

Lighting at the Railway, which is also excellent, is performed by two local men, Bob Aylott from North Harrow and John Jenkins from Pinner This light show normally travels with the Inside System, another local group.

Rock music is undergoing a strong revival trend and it looks as if Saturday nights at the Railway Hotel will go down very well — much to the satisfaction of Johnny Quantrell and the Confederates.

THE HARROW OBSERVER MAY 1ST 1970

THE ROCKHOUSE (1971)

The Rockhouse was a short-lived Rock club on a Thursday night at the Railway Hotel that very soon moved to the Roxborough pub in Harrow. See Screaming Lord Sutch section above.

THE KIWI CLUB

The Kiwi Club was a Reggae and Soul club that operated at the Railway Hotel on Friday nights during 1972. As you can see from the local newspaper report from October 1972 it was not without its troubles!

THINGS WENT CRAZY AT KIWI CLUB

WHEN POLICE RAIDED the Crazy Kiwi Club at the Railway Hotel, Wealdstone, on Friday, a fracas broke out among several men, Harrow Court heard on Tuesday.

ROCK AND ROLL NIGHTS (1998)

In 1998 Rock'N'Roll returned to the Railway Hotel in the form of a Disco hosted by 'Fifties Flash' or if you prefer Keith from Pinner! A brief return for Keith who used to perform the same duties almost thirty years before!

Rockers turn back clock to the Fifties

■ WEALDSTONE: Rock 'n' roll returns to The Railway Hotel on Friday nights tomorrow — with the pub's original Sixties disc jockey at the turntables. "I'll be playing a broad church of music, from the pre-Presley era, 1949, up to about 1962," said Fifties Flash, also known as Keith, from Pinner Road,

THE EZEE CLUB

The Ezee Club was a short-lived Beat club that opened at the Railway Hotel in February 1962.

THE BOOM ROOM

The Boom Room was a short-lived venture that saw up and coming Blues bands playing at the Railway Hotel on Friday nights in late 1963. However, it was not a great success and the plug was pulled on it by the end of the year!

THURSDAY BLUES CLUB

In July 1968 the Thursday Blues club which had been operating at the Tithe Farm (Rayners Lane F.C.) relocated for whatever reason to the Railway Hotel. Membership cards from the previous venue were honoured and it was able to attract some very big names. The flyer below shows details of its first few weeks at its new home.

TUESDAY BLUES CLUB / BALDRY'S BLUES CLUB/ BLUESDAY R'N'B CLUB

As reported in a previous section Cyril Davies was a pioneer of British Blues, and started a very successful Blues club in late 1962 at the Railway Hotel. Initially Cyril Davies used it as a vehicle for his own band but soon diversified. When Davies died in 1964 his ex-bandmate Long John Baldry very soon took over the reins and renamed it after himself! This later became the Bluesday Rhythm and Blues club, which was when The Who made their debut at the Railway Hotel.

TUESDAY NIGHT IS RHYTHM N'BLUES NIGHT

The Railway Hotel, Harrow Wealdstone

OPENING 11th DECEMBER.

Cyril Davies and the All-Star R & B Band

3/6d.

Free Membership Opening Night.

IRISH DANCING CLUBS

There were known to be many Irish Dancing Clubs that appeared or rehearsed at the Railway Hotel over the years, including Hickeys Irish Dancing Team during the seventies.

DISCO'S/KARAOKE

There have been many Discos' and Karaoke's over the years at the Railway Hotel, both upstairs and downstairs. Perhaps, none remembered more than the legendary Robin and Paul aka 'Pinky and Perky' who were at countless events in the later years of the Railway, as well as starting a successful Gay night on Wednesdays.

KARAOKE NIGHTS

Bookings for all occasions
Pubs, Clubs and private Parties
★ Compere and 2 Video Screens ★
Over 600 songs to choose from
For the most competitive prices

Tel: 0923 249864

ask for JOHN or JUNE

Come along on Sunday Nights
★ The Railway Hotel ★
Harrow Weald (on the Bridge)
Bar open 7pm 'til Midnight • Doors close at 9.45

AN ADVERT FOR JOHN AND JUNE'S SUNDAY NIGHT DISCO'S IN 1991

LUV SHACK OVER 30s DISCO PARTY

EVERY MONDAY

at the Railway Hotel
By Harrow and Wealdstone Station
Harrow, 8.30 till 12.30
Smart dress – No jeans or trainers

FREE ADMISSION FOR LADIES ON 8th JULY BEFORE 9.30PM

AN OVER 30'S DISCO IN 1996

DELL RICHARDSON

Dell Richardson was a well-known local Rock'N'Roll DJ who played at many venues in the area including the Railway Hotel in the seventies and eighties. In 1998 Dell joined Radio Caroline and can still be heard on it to this day.

SAVE OUR SOLES DISCO

Cleaning up the Disco scene

ENTERPRISING determination is almost a rare quality these days, but two determined young lads from Cambridge Road, North Harrow, are showing their metal in launching a complete disco unit; complete that is with publicity machinery and bouncers, called Save our Souls disco, using the re-vamped Railway Hotel, Wealdstone, as a possible permanent Thursday night venue, starting March 25.

Mark Slater, 19-year-old, and Craig Williams (21), who launched their first official evening at the Headstone Hotel last week (to an audience of about 350), have been working together for about three months doing private parties and things. But they want to launch out.

Now they hire a hall, publicise the event and supply all the bouncers and services necessary for a disco at whatever venue they can get, whether a hall, a pub room or a hotel.

"There are so many discos going round, but there are not that many good ones, so we want to try and change that", Mark told the Observer. "Craig has worked at Circles, and at the Birdnest as it used to be called, and I have done a fair bit, so we are experienced. We have about 2,500 records between us that we have been collecting over the past couple of years, so we thought we should put them to good use."

Besides playing soul, predominantly American soul, (hardly surprising as that is the home if you really mean good soul) Mark does a fine dress-up and dance-around type live show, so he said, and all in all, it sounds like a show with a difference, based on good solid music.

The boys started out with a Friday date at the Railway — a weekly event if it proves popular — and they return to the Headstone on April 3. They hope the venture turns out OK. Obviously finances are important when you are paying a retainer for the hall and taking profits — you have to be good to stay alive in that business. Time will tell, as they say.

THE HARROW OBSERVER DATED 9TH MARCH 1976

THEY ALSO SERVED!

There are, of course, many names missing from the above, some have just disappeared, some can't be remembered and some despite many fruitless attempts have just remained elusive! My extreme apologies to anybody whose name is omitted, but rest assured your part in the history of the Railway Hotel was every bit as important as the previously mentioned names.

Here are, however, a few names to mull over of various acts that I know definitely played the Railway Hotel, but alas I have been unable to find out any details about them!

CHAPTER – PLAYED IN THE 70'S.

DISCO 2 - ? MAY 1970.

THE EXTRAVAGANZA BANDWAGONERS – PLAYED IN 1962.

FAMOUS SEAMUS (IRISH VOCALIST) – PLAYED IN THE 90'S.

GOOD EARTH – PLAYED IN THE 70'S.

THE HAARLEMS – 17TH AUGUST 1969.

THE HELICOPTERS – 2ND JANUARY 1979.

THE IMPALAS – (NOT TO BE CONFUSED WITH AMERICAN BAND OF SAME NAME) PLAYED IN THE 70'S.

BEN E. JAMES (SOUL BAND) – PLAYED IN THE 70'S.

THE LEGEND – 2ND MAY 1970.

THE MEMFIS BAND – PLAYED IN THE 70'S?

METROPOLITAN GREASE FORCE (ROCK'N'ROLL BAND) – PLAYED IN THE 70'S.

PEGASUS BLUES – 8TH AUGUST 1968.

ROY POWELL ROCK'N'ROLL BAND – PLAYED IN THE 70'S.

THE RATIO SHOWBAND – 6TH JULY 1969.

RAY AND THE ROADSHOW – 24TH AUGUST 1970.

BARON RAY SOUND – DJ FROM THE 70'S.

ROCK 'N'ROLL EXPRESS (ROCK'N'ROLL BAND) – PLAYED IN THE 70'S.

SOUL COMMITTEE (SOUL BAND) – 25TH AUGUST 1968.

SOUND INJECTION – 14TH JUNE 1997.

THE WHO
aka THE HIGH NUMBERS

Mention the Railway Hotel and the very strong likelihood is that the name of The Who will very soon crop up, was there a more famous band to grace the old venue? Certainly none were to leave their mark (literally) on the Railway Hotel in quite the same way as the 'Orrible Oo'.

The Who started life as The Detours, but this name was changed due to the fact another band was also using it at the time. The Who was very much Roger Daltrey's band in the early days, and it was him who called the shots. Bolstered by two ex-school mates (although mates might have been stretching it a bit – they were certainly all aware of each other at school), John Entwistle and Pete Townshend they were completed by Doug Sandom on drums. Doug Sandom was a few years older than the rest of the band and this and a culmination of other things eventually saw him being replaced by Keith Moon!

A YOUNG PETE TOWNSHEND AT THE RAILWAY HOTEL IN JULY 1964

Technically most of the bands appearances at the Railway Hotel were as The High Numbers due to Pete Meaden the manager of the band at the time urging them to change to a more 'mod friendly' moniker! Richard Barnes (a flat mate and Art Student friend of Pete Townshend) had started co-promoting a new version of the Tuesday Rhythm and Blues night called the Bluesday R'N'B club. The aim was to make it a rallying point for the growing Mod contingent in the area, in fact by just the second week the road outside the Railway was already knee deep in Lambretta's and Vespa's, and their new found heroes had just released their first single!

In the 2014 film entitled' Lambert and Stamp', Richard Barnes took up the story:-

'I ran this club it was the Railway Hotel and it was a real dump – really, it was a basement of a pub. It was there that Kit lambert was driving along and saw outside this whole line of scooters, Vespa's and Lambretta's parked everywhere, and Mods in Parkas talking, he was intrigued because he was looking for a band to include in a film that he and his partner Chris Stamp wanted to do!

He came down and this guy said to me there's a guy outside in a suit, a very official looking bloke, and we were worried that we were going to get caught for having too many people. Lambert said he looked in the club and it looked like a version of Hell! He said it was all dark, and he said he immediately knew that was the band he had been looking for, because there were all these Mods watching Moon go mad, and they were great!'

The above event happened on 14th July 1964, and the excited Lambert was eager for Stamp to witness what he had seen. Stamp was away in Ireland filming at the time, but caught a future performance a fortnight later in nearby Watford and was similarly hooked. Things took a rapid turn of events with the planned filming of the band taking place a few weeks later on 11th August 1964. Ultimately, Lambert and Stamp would wrestle for the right to manage their new find, although it would be a helter skelter ride that was to see them replaced some years later following Roger Daltrey's insistence that they should be sacked for various 'misdemeanours'.

For the record The Who's residency at the Railway Hotel was as follows:-

Tuesday 30th June 1964	the start of a twelve week stint, with a set including breaks lasting from 8.00pm until 1.00am.
Tuesday 7th July 1964	although billed as The Who they were in fact The High Numbers at this stage. The band had just released their first single (3 days before) which was billed as the first authentic Mod record!

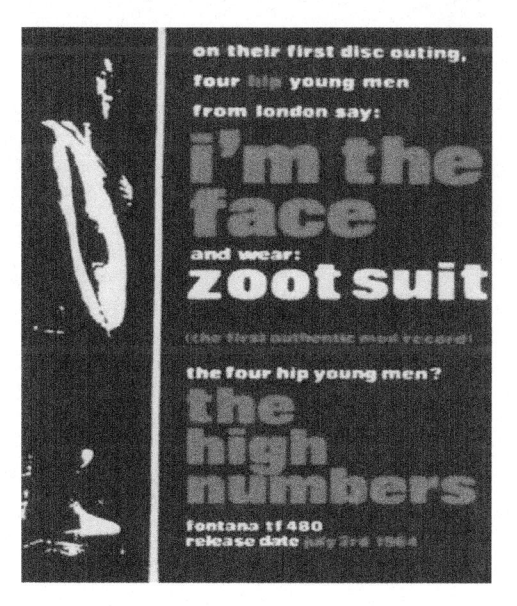

Tuesday 14th July 1964	the day that was to change everything for The Who (although still The High Numbers as a certain Kit Lambert was in attendance!
Tuesday 21st July 1964	billed as The High Numbers (formerly The Who)
Tuesday 28th July 1964	a set that lasted from 8pm until 11pm.
Tuesday 4th August 1964	a set that lasted from 8pm until 11pm.
Tuesday 11th August 1964	a set that lasted from 8pm until 11pm and was filmed for prosperity by Kit Lambert and Chris Stamp. Also note the dark glasses worn by Roger Daltrey.
Tuesday 18th August 1964	a set that lasted from 8pm until 11pm.
Tuesday 25th August 1964	a set that lasted from 8pm until 11pm, and for some reason the last gig at the Railway Hotel for a couple of weeks. The following Tuesday they were replaced by Gary Farr and the T-bone's.
Tuesday 8th September 1964	a set that lasted from 8pm until 11pm.
Tuesday 15th September 1964	penultimate appearance at the Railway Hotel for The High Numbers.
Tuesday 22nd September 1964	the last date of a twelve week residency comes to an end.

BELOW COPIES OF TWO ADVERTS FROM THE MELODY MAKER DATED 4TH AND 11TH JULY 1964

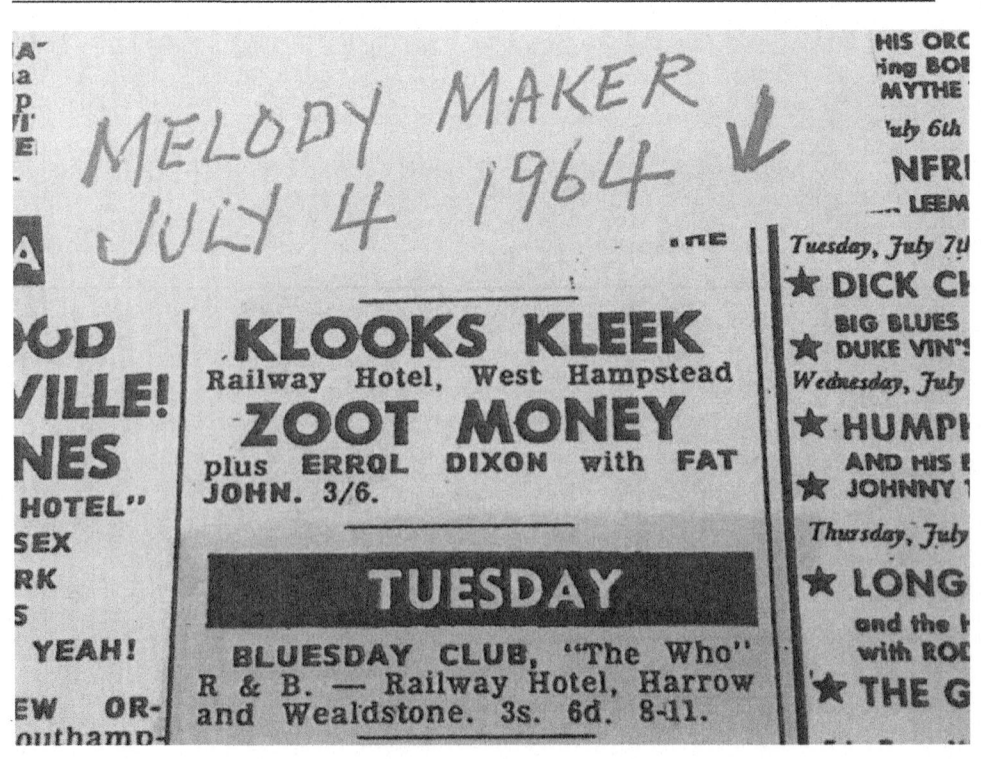

MELODY MAKER JULY 4 1964

KLOOKS KLEEK
Railway Hotel, West Hampstead
ZOOT MONEY
plus ERROL DIXON with FAT JOHN. 3/6.

TUESDAY
BLUESDAY CLUB, "The Who"
R & B. — Railway Hotel, Harrow and Wealdstone. 3s. 6d. 8-11.

NOTE THE BAND BILLED AS THE WHO IN ONE AND THE HIGH NUMBERS IN THE FOLLOWING!

GRATEFUL THANKS FOR THESE IS EXTENDED TO THE PERSONAL ARCHIVES OF 'IRISH JACK'

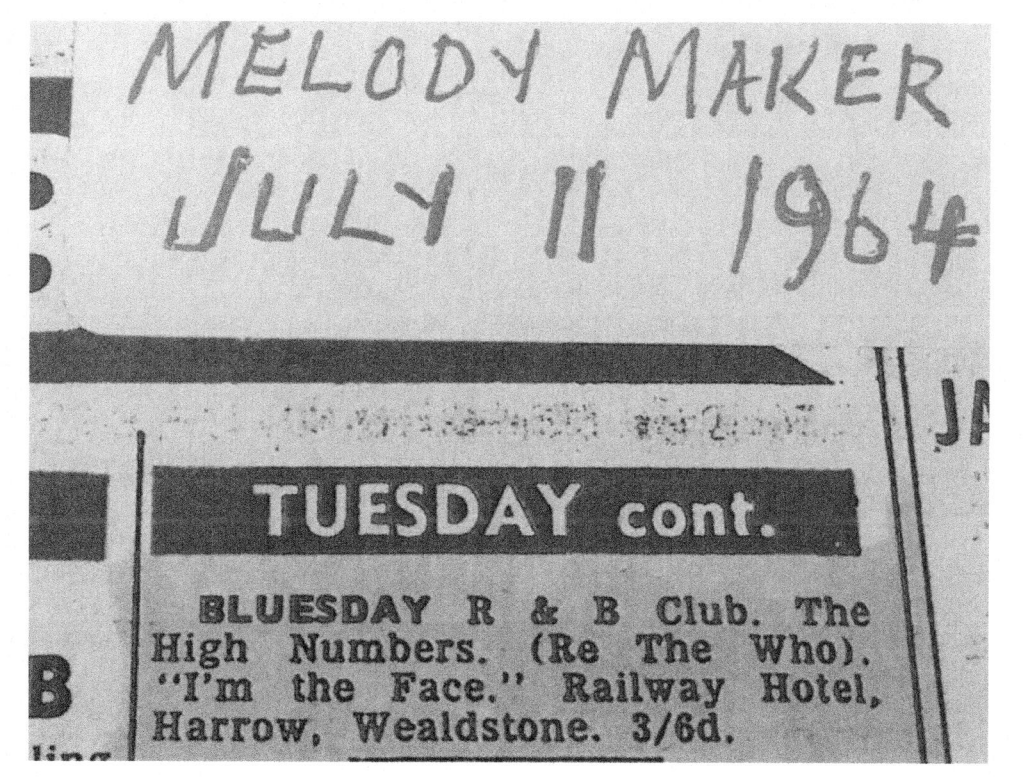

MELODY MAKER JULY 11 1964

TUESDAY cont.

BLUESDAY R & B Club. The High Numbers. (Re The Who). "I'm the Face." Railway Hotel, Harrow, Wealdstone. 3/6d.

> ★ **"SENSATIONAL - WEIRD!"**
>
> ★ **BACK BY POPULAR DEMAND!**
>
> # THE WHO!
>
> **THIS SUNDAY, FEB 14th**
> Railway Hotel Harrow & Wealdstone

THE ABOVE FLYER FROM 1965 LOOKS LIKELY TO HAVE BEEN CANCELLED FOR SOME REASON!

PETE TOWNSHED STARTS A VERY EXPENSIVE TRADITION

If every person who claims to have been there the night that Pete Townshend smashed his Rickenbacker for the very first time the Railway Hotel would have been many hundreds beyond it safe and legal capacity! A lost in time 'I was there moment', people can't even agree the date that Townshend's expensive new hobby started.

Many people claim that it was either Tuesday 8th or Tuesday 16th September 1964, with the man himself categorically stating that it occurred at the first show he played there on Tuesday 30th June 1964! In his fantastic autobiography, Who I Am published by Harper Collins in 2012 Townshend opens his memoirs relating the story thus:-

'Usually I'd be feeling like a loner, even in the middle of the band, but tonight, in June 1964, at The Who's first show at the Railway Hotel in Harrow, West London, I am invincible.

We're playing R&B: 'Smokestack Lightning', 'I'm a Man', 'Road Runner' and other heavy classics. I scrape the howling Rickenbacker guitar up and down my microphone stand, then flip the special switch I recently fitted so the guitar splutters and sprays the front row with bullets of sound. I violently thrust my guitar into the air – and feel a terrible shudder as the sound goes from a roar to a rattling growl; I look up to see my guitar's broken head as I pull it away from the hole I've punched in the low ceiling.

It is at this moment that I make a split-second decision – and in a mad frenzy I thrust the damaged guitar up into the ceiling over and over again. What had been a clean break becomes a splintered mess. I hold the guitar up to the crowd triumphantly. I haven't smashed it: I've sculpted it for them.'

The great man's account is highly plausible as the notoriously low ceiling would have been no stranger to him by September so I will go with him on this! After paying for the ceiling to be repaired all future damage tended to be inflicted on his own equipment! And so began a very costly tradition that would follow Pete Townshend around for many years. The crowd would be disappointed if Townshend didn't engage in what he called 'auto destructive art', and add to the equation that Keith Moon also felt the need to join in, it's a wonder they made any money at all in the early days! Townshend's trade mark guitar smashing would soon be mimicked by all and sundry, including the likes of Jimmi Hendrix!

A true piece of Rock folklore had been born and it happened first in the good old Railway Hotel!

DALTREY AND THE RUMBLE IN THE CAR PARK

On the August 11th 1964 with The High Numbers returning to the Railway Hotel for their first filmed recording, things didn't go quite as planned for Roger Daltrey. Daltrey had seemingly had somewhat of a domestic with his new wife before heading off to the performance! Just prior to the band going on stage Daltrey's father-in-law dragged him outside in to the car-park, a fight ensued and Daltrey was forced to hide a wounded eye with dark glasses.

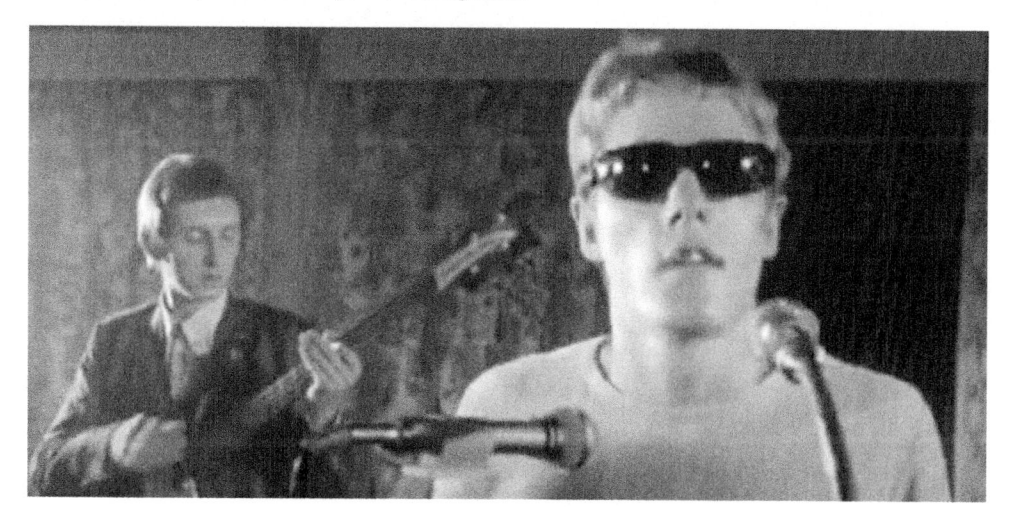

MEATY BEATY BIG AND BOUNCY

For many years in the upstairs bar of the Railway Hotel a crudely framed cover of an LP by The Who hung with little or no fanfare. It was in fact the 1971 album of the above name, which was a compilation of many of the bands greatest hits, all of which were released after the group had played at the Railway Hotel for the last time! The album done very well for The Who and peaked at Number 9 in the UK album charts, the track listing is as follows:-

1. I Can't Explain
2. The Kids Are Alright
3. Happy Jack
4. I Can See for Miles
5. Pictures of Lily
6. My Generation
7. The Seeker
8. Anyway, Anyhow, Anywhere
9. Pinball Wizard
10. A Legal Matter
11. Boris the Spider
12. Magic Bus
13. Substitute
14. I'm a Boy

The iconic gatefold sleeve was photographed by Graham Hughes and designed by Mike Shaw and Bill Curbishley. Curbishley would later (and is still to this day) become the Manager of The Who, his brother Paul is one of the four young lads featured on the cover and would later have a brief career as a professional footballer with West ham United, the other brother Alan would also follow that route but with a much higher degree of success!

The inner sleeve pictured over was photographed in 1971 and mocked up to look as if it was taken in 1965. A poster shows that The Who will play there on Sunday May 18th 1965, in reality the band were actually in Swindon on that date, and had long since finished their residency at the Railway Hotel. The historical inaccuracies aside Meaty Beaty Big and Bouncy is a great memento of a golden time in the history of both the Railway Hotel and The Who.

THE INSIDE OF THE GATEFOLD COVER OF MEATY BEATY BIG AND BOUNCY

Youth '71

Meaty Beaty Big and Bouncy Railway Rockhouse is centre of Who's latest LP

Fresh paint has now covered up the atmosphere which made the picture (left) effective, but it is still recognisable as Wealdstone's centre of rock and roll, and the discotheque where The Who played before they rose to fame.

The picture is from The Who's latest LP, "Meaty Beaty Big and Bouncy," which has already sold 20,000 copies.

The Who played at the Railway Hotel, Wealdstone, in 1964, and the LP has all the best of The Who, with "Happy Jack," "I'm A Boy," "Substitute" and "Pinball Wizard," just some of the tracks.

It is already in the LP charts.

OBSERVER AND GAZETTE Friday, December 31, 1971

THE WHO AT THE RAILWAY ON CD AND FILM

At least two recordings are available of The Who's performance at the Railway Hotel on 11th August 1964 (?) both are unofficial bootlegs – but easily obtainable on line.

The first CD pictured above was released by Yellow Dog Records in 2002 and also features a studio session thought to be at Abbey Road in October 1964, however, the later I am extremely sceptical about! What I am definitely sure of is that this CD has a serious floor in stating that it was a live recording by The High Numbers at the Railway Hotel on 20th October 1964 The High Numbers changed their name back to The Who around then! Also, they did not play at the Railway Hotel on that date, and there is even a suggestion (and confirmed by an expert in these matters) that the instrumental music is by another band! The most likely situation is that The Who/ The High Numbers confirmed songs were recorded as per the next CD on 11th August 1964. Still it is a great and easily obtainable record of their time at the Railway Hotel and available on eBay for around £10. The track listing for the above is as follows:-

1. I Gotta Dance To Keep From Crying

2. You Really Got Me (Instrumental – by?)

3. Young Man Blues

4. Green Onions

5. I Gotta Dance to Keep From Crying

6. Jam (Instrumental – by?)

7. I Gotta Dance to Keep From Crying

8. Long Tall Shorty

9. Pretty Thing

10. Smokestack Lightning - Money (That's What I Want)

11. Here 'Tis

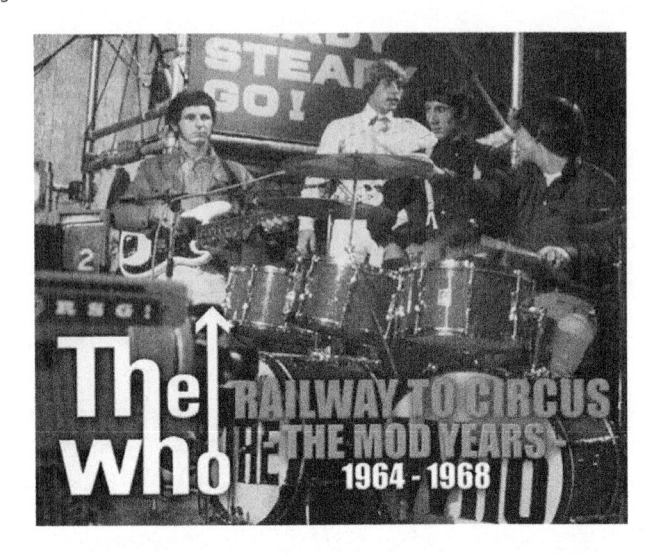

The Railway to Circus is a double CD and DVD package from TOMMY Records released in 2003, quite a rare recording expect to pay in excess of £50! The package includes the following set list from 11th August 1964:-

1. I Gotta Dance To Keep From Crying

2. Ooh Poo Pah Doo - LONG VERSION

3. I Gotta Dance to Keep From Crying #1

4. You Really Got Me (cuts in)

5. Young Man Blues (cuts in at beginning)

6. . Green Onions (cuts in)

7. I Gotta Dance to Keep From Crying #2

8. Instrumental Jam

9. I Gotta Dance To Keep From Crying

10. Long Tall Shorty

11. Pretty Thing (cuts in)

12. Smokestack Lightning - Money (That's What I Want) (cuts in)

13. Here 'Tis (incomplete)

The package also includes footage of a couple of the above on its DVD, and further live recordings from various other locations.

The docu/film entitled Lambert and Stamp was released in 2014 and is a very good record of the early days of The Who, and features all that remains of the footage shot by Lambert and Stamp at the Railway Hotel. The great footage which is just under eight minutes long was lost and presumed lost for nearly forty years! The remaining footage features 'Ooh Poo Pah Doo' and then cuts into 'Got to Dance to Keep From Crying'. The footage features many locals, with some great dance moves, although one young couple are completely oblivious and dance slowly as if the band are singing a ballad! Another great image is of a young lad swilling his pint as he dances away without a care in the world. Readily available on Youtube it's definitely worth a watch! Originally over forty minute's footage was shot on 16mm film stock.

SOME OF THE PEOPLE PACKED INTO THE RAILWAY HOTEL TO SEE THE WHO/HIGH NUMBERS

KEITH MOON APPEARING WITH THE WHO/HIGH NUMBERS – HE HAD ACTUALLY ALREADY PLAYED THE VENUE WITH HIS PREVIOUS BAND – THE BEACHCOMBERS!

YOUNG MODS ARE CAPTIVATED BY THE DRUMMING OF KEITH MOON – JULY 1964

THE WHO REMEMBERED AT THE RAILWAY

Of course, it has already been noted what an intrinsic part of the Railway Hotel's history is forever linked to The Who, and in 2004 the flats that now occupy the old site were christened Daltry and Moon House respectively. Sadly someone decided to misspell the name of the lead singer leaving out an all-important 'e'! Also poor old Townshend and Entwistle received no such honour! In 2009 a plaque was initialised by the local council which was in an out of the way location, and ripe for removal by a souvenir hunter. Predictably the plaque was duly stolen, and has never been replaced, in fact when I contacted a couple of the local councillors to float the idea of its replacement it was seemingly deemed unworthy of a reply!

THE PLAQUE THAT BRIEFLY REMAINED AT THE FORMER SITE OF THE RAILWAY HOTEL BEFORE BEING STOLEN

The Who get plaque at pub where Pete Townshend wrecked his first guitar

A plaque has gone up in the Railway Hotel, North London, where The Who's axeman Pete Townshend wrecked his first guitar in 1964!

THE DAILY MIRROR DECEMBER 2009

REMEMBERING THE RAILWAY

Special memories of Christmas Day, hot toddies and cigar from Derry Hipwell as a welcome!

DAVE BARRATT – former regular at The Railway and Wealdstone Social Club

Screaming Lord Sutch used to come to fund raising events you would never meet a nicer man. We all loved him. He once gave me a tip, a £1Million pound note, and where the Queens head should be, was his.

LUCY CHALLIS – Barmaid at the Railway Hotel for 15 years

Sunday nights were always special. The Connolly Folk Band playing I think they might also have been called Saisoire. Usually packed, they used to play Flower of Scotland for Andy and Brian. Happy days!

DAVE BARRATT – former regular at The Railway and Wealdstone Social Club

In the 80's Liverpool always seemed to be in a cup final at Wembley. The fans would arrive in their coaches, park up in the civic centre car park, and head for us. We were always so excited, we loved the Liverpool fans. You'd arrive for work and there would be red shirts as far as the eye could see. Once we opened up, they'd stream through the doors, singing all the football songs. They'd hang their flags all over the pub. They were the best fans you could wish for! They were suffering the recession at the time, but that was one day of the year, they celebrated, win or lose! They'd sing the whole session, and then off they went to Wembley. They always came back after the match and had one for the road. We never had any trouble they were great people!

LUCY CHALLIS – Barmaid at the Railway Hotel for 15 years

LUCY CHALLIS ON THE RIGHT WITH FELLOW BARMAID CARA

I started picking glasses up when I was 13 and Dennis was the boss, Brendan came when I was 15 I remember seeing Kevin Rowland from Dexys Midnight Runners there once or twice!

SHAUN GLOADY – Potboy/Barman and long-time customer at the Railway

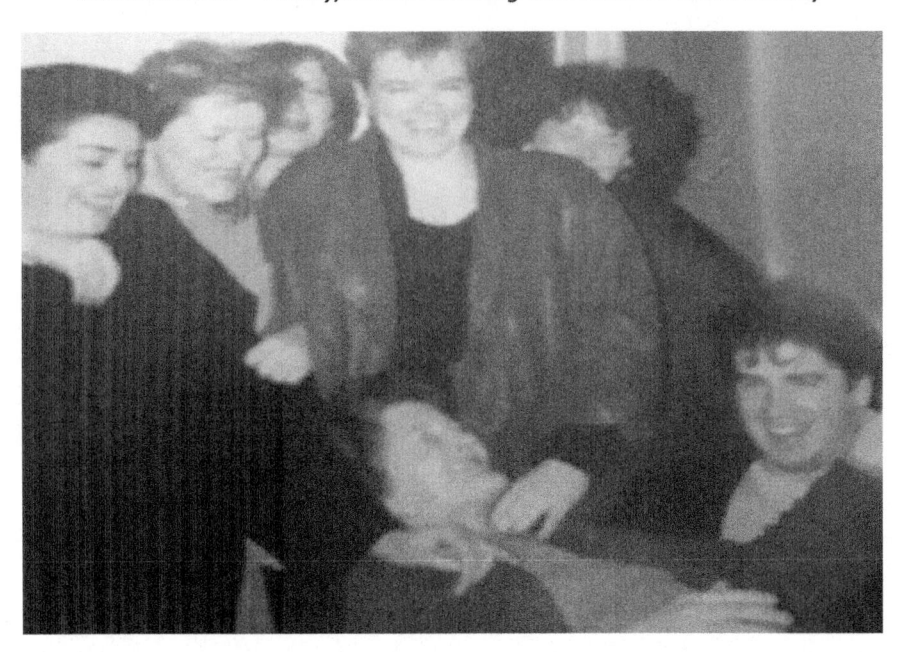

<u>**SHAUN AND COMPANY JUST PRIOR TO ANOTHER NIGHT AT THE RAILWAY c1990**</u>

<u>**PHOTOGRAPH COURTESY – DEIRDRE MAHER**</u>

<u>**THE VICTORIOUS RAILWAY F.C. – CELEBRATING A LEAGUE CHAMPIONSHIP**</u>

That was a very decent side, a lot of players who were in and around the Rayners Lane first team at the time. Roland Matthews, Reg Barton, Darrell Clements, Charlie Morris, Steve Frimley, Tony Kiely. Also a few in there in case the opposition fancied it.

GORDON McKAY – Former player with the Railway F.C. and lifelong Wealdstone Fan

1976ish I saw a band at the Railway who had just changed their name to Racing Cars; they sang their new song – They Shoot Horses Don't They? Next thing I know they are on the bloody Top of the Pops and it was in the chart for ages!

PETE BURROWS – Former resident and local councillor from Wealdstone

A sad end to a great venue! We (The Beachcombers) played a few gigs there, and also used to rehearse there on Sunday mornings.

JOHN SCHOLLAR – Former band mate of Keith Moon

We all went there as kids.... and me more than others! I am in this film as a very shy and retiring (or should I say hiding being scared to be there) because of my age and my father, a police man would have killed me! I can't remember the name of the film.

CYNTHIA PRENTICE – Former Regular at The Who concerts at the Railway Hotel as featured in the Lambert and Stamp film

I used to work at Hamilton's (Huzzah!) and meet my girlfriend who worked at the Civic Centre for lunch. I went to see a couple of bands down at the Sidings, which was great. Tudors 'night club' just over the road with a mainline connection made it very popular I remember I used to meet folk from all over London.

JENNY TAILER – Local who used to attend gigs at the Railway Hotel

As a child I used to visit my Nan and Mum who worked in the kitchen, I remember the biggest table I'd ever seen, and sitting on it as my Nan cooked, my Mum did some cleaning. I also used to sit in the bar on a high stall with Lemonade. My Nans name was Ivy Tyler and my Mum Helen Tyler.

DEBBIE WEBB – Former Wealdstone Resident

I frequented the "Lounge Bar" during the seventies. Only went downstairs once or twice and stayed well clear of the public bar!

COLIN LESLIE – Former customer

I first started to work there when my Dad Phil was running the Dance down stairs; Uncle Jim and Pat Gloady and Johnny Linehan were the bouncers as well as many other! All very tough guys in their day - brave and fearless. I started by taking the money at the door, after a while (still under age) went to work in the bar still down stairs, Mum took over the door money and Aunty Bernie did the cloak room. One of the bouncers Dave got an axe in his stomach in the car park one night but thankfully recovered!

PHILIPPA GLOADY – Former employee and customer

I worked for 3 years as head barman in the Railway, my wife also worked there as a barmaid. Great old community pub (I've been running Frostys in Kenton for the past 3 years) everyone still talks about the Railway it was the hub of the community and sadly never replaced. Wealdstone died when the Railway closed!

PHILLIP PARSONS – Head Barman at the Railway during the Hipwell era

I worked at Harrow Magistrate's Court in the early 80's and spent many a lunchtime in the Railway, as well as celebrations and leaving do's after work in there with colleagues and friends. Then across the road and down the steps that took me to the bus stop and my journey home. The immediate memory that springs to mind is being in there one lunchtime and playing the slot machine with a friend during our lunch hour. The machine got stuck and was paying out something like 2:1 for every 10p we got 20p back. I thought this was a useful bit of extra cash and repeatedly placed my bet knowing I was certain of leaving with more than I arrived with, albeit slow but sure. My colleague preferred to live dangerously, quickly became disillusioned with our good fortune and pressed the "clear" button. I was furious!

KIM LEACH – Former lunchtime customer

Living in Wealdstone my gang often went to the Railway for the evening and one Friday The High Numbers were down to appear. Entrance was 7/6d (35pence) and in 1965 you could get seriously drunk for a week on that, and have change for 10 fags! We paid up, endured them for half an hour, drank up, agreed they'd never make it and went off, possibly to the Dominion or Granada flicks or gate-crash some poor sods party. A month later they were on Ready Steady GO on Friday night as The Who and the rest is history as they say.

I was a Mod at the time (72 this month) all Carnaby Street, tab collar shirt and Lambrettas so they and The Small Faces were my kind of British band along with the American West Coast sounds like the Byrds & Sonny & Cher. Out of interest Roger Daltrey, who sang "I hope I die before I get old" now runs a trout fishery (or did) in Kent and used to shop at the same store as my wife's sister who said he was a real gentleman and always pleasant to talk to. Also as an aside, I used to deliver fruit and greengrocery items on an old tradesman's bike with a cage at the front wheel to the Railway when I was 11 years old then zoom down the steep slope alongside and up Marlborough Hill!

STUART HAMMOND – Former Mod who saw The Who at the Railway when appearing as The High Numbers

I was a regular at the Railway in 62/63 in the "Boom Room." Long John Baldry & The Hoochie Coochie Men, renamed from "Cyril Davies All Stars" after he died, played Sunday nights with Rod Stewart doing occasional vocals. They were replaced by The Bo Street Runners. A friend of mine, with Dick Barnes, started "Tuesday Blues" featuring "The Who." They dropped the "High Numbers" name when they started playing the Railway. I met with Keith Moon outside of the Railway a couple of times and met his parents. I used to run the cloakroom at Tuesday Blues charging sixpence for each mod girls handbag. I also drove around with Barnes & friends pasting up fly posters all over Harrow to promote the gigs. Also went to several social events, usually organized by the YCL or YCND.

JOHN BUTLER – Former regular at The Who (and other) gigs at the Railway

We used to go to the Railway on a Friday night as well as Sunday night where you could see the High Numbers (The Who) as well as many other up & coming groups! On one particular Friday night 22nd Nov 63 we were on our way to the Boom Room which was the cellar where The Who often played when we heard that President Kennedy had been assassinated, kind of sticks in the mind the history of that day! Many times we would be at the front of the Railway on our scooters especially Sunday evenings, great days, great times, and great music!

JOHN PATTERSON – (my uncle) and former attendee of Mod gigs at the Railway Hotel

When I was younger my dad and his friends used the Railway for the pigeon club called the greater Harrow racing pigeon club on most Friday nights. I have very fond memories of my childhood there!

ALAN BROWN – Former Wealdstone resident and businessman

Well, The Railway, where do I start? This played a major part in my life from my late teens. I and my sister Mary started using the pub as our good friend Shaun started working there at weekends. Most Friday's we would go there between 9:30/10.00pm we would go at that time as we knew we would end up downstairs at "The Sidings" until it closed at 2am (probably nearer 3 by the time you'd finished your drinks and said your goodbyes). We met two other sisters (who we didn't like the look of at first and vice versa) but, eventually we got talking and they were Scottish, they were Senga & Joanie Harvey. We became very good friends and would meet there every weekend from then on in. Every other Saturday, I used to travel to Manchester, to watch the "Mighty United" with my Dad and Layne Patterson. I wouldn't get home until about 9:30 in the evening, so it would be a quick bath/shower, get changed and hopefully be down the Railway by 10:30 at the latest to meet Mary, Senga and Joanie. I met a lot of other good friends down there, a lot of them were bar staff who we met through Shaun, there was Michael & Stephen Hipwell (whose Parents Derry & Pat ran the Railway) Mandy who started dating Michael H and were later married, Patsy L, Martina, Laura, Patsy H, Mary F (all Bar staff) Mick B & Steve F. A week or so before Christmas we would have Christmas Dinner downstairs in the pub (The Sidings) which was arranged and cooked by Mandy & Michael. One of the day's we had the dinner it fell on my birthday (14th Dec), and as a present they bought me a "Blow up Doll", which Shaun and Laura had taken to the garage across the road to get blown up, I can only imagine the look's they got! By the end of the evening after a lot of partying, the doll was quite deflated, and partied out (as were most of us) great times!

DEIRD' A LIFELONG MANCHESTER UNITED FAN ATTEMPTS TO CONVERT A VISITING LIVERPOOL FAN AT THE RAILWAY c1985

I was called the evening the Railway was on fire. I went down there with another good friend of mine (Sally) who also was a regular with us down there, and we watched it burn with tears running down our cheeks. I had so many great times at the Railway and made some lifelong friends. We still try and get together for drinks a few times a year. Those are only a couple of memories from the many 100's I have of my time in the Railway. Brilliant place and greatly missed by many.

DEIRDRE MAHER – regular at the Railway Hotel during the 80's and 90's

I had some fantastic nights there – above and below. The best Rock and Roll venue in 'Arra!

BOB K – former regular at the Railway Hotel

Another memory from the Railway was that you had to dress smart to go down "The Sidings" which meant the men would have to wear "Trousers not Jeans".

My brother John would always wear trousers anyway, so when he used to go down the sidings with his mates, John would go in first, go to the toilet, take his trousers off, pass them out the toilet window to one of his mates to put on, so he could get in too! This would go on several times until they were all in!

DEIRDRE MAHER – regular at the Railway Hotel during the 80's and 90's

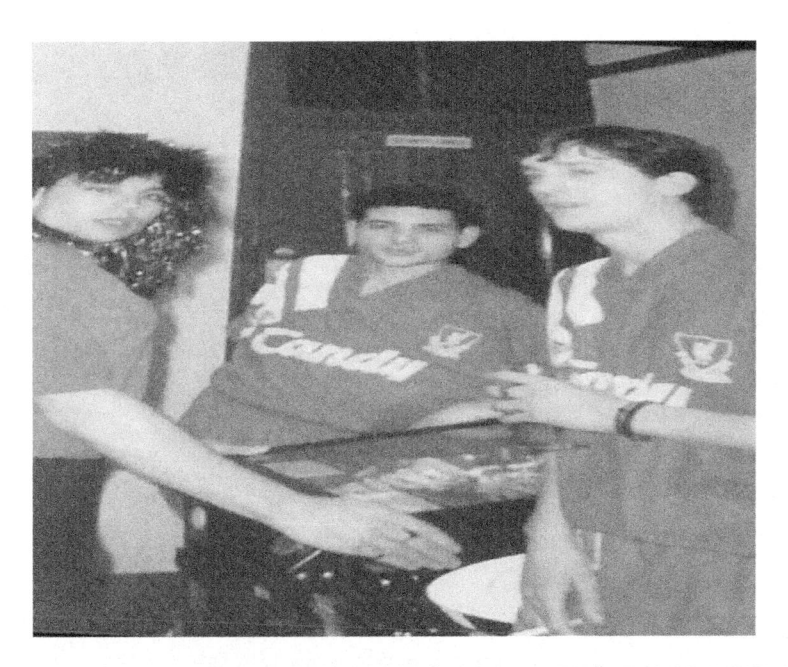

ANOTHER INVASION OF LIVERPOOL SUPPORTERS (KENTON BASED!) AT THE RAILWAY HOTEL FRASER (IN THE FEMALE WIG) AND MARK GREIG, ALONGSIDE JAMIE NORMAN c 1992. PIC COURTESY – DEIRDRE MAHER

I was the best man at a mates wedding reception there. Shirley Eaton (who lived in Derby Avenue) and had been at Whitfriars School was there with Max Bygraves.

JIM H – Best Man at a Railway Hotel wedding

I spent my youth in the Railway Hotel. It was the first pub I went to when I arrived in Harrow. Spent every weekend in the Sidings and the resident band came back to the house we were renting and played the night of my birthday! Neighbours were not impressed!! Great memories going there every weekend with the bar staff from Wealdstone Social Club.

CAROLINE RYDER – Former Stewardess at Wealdstone Social Club

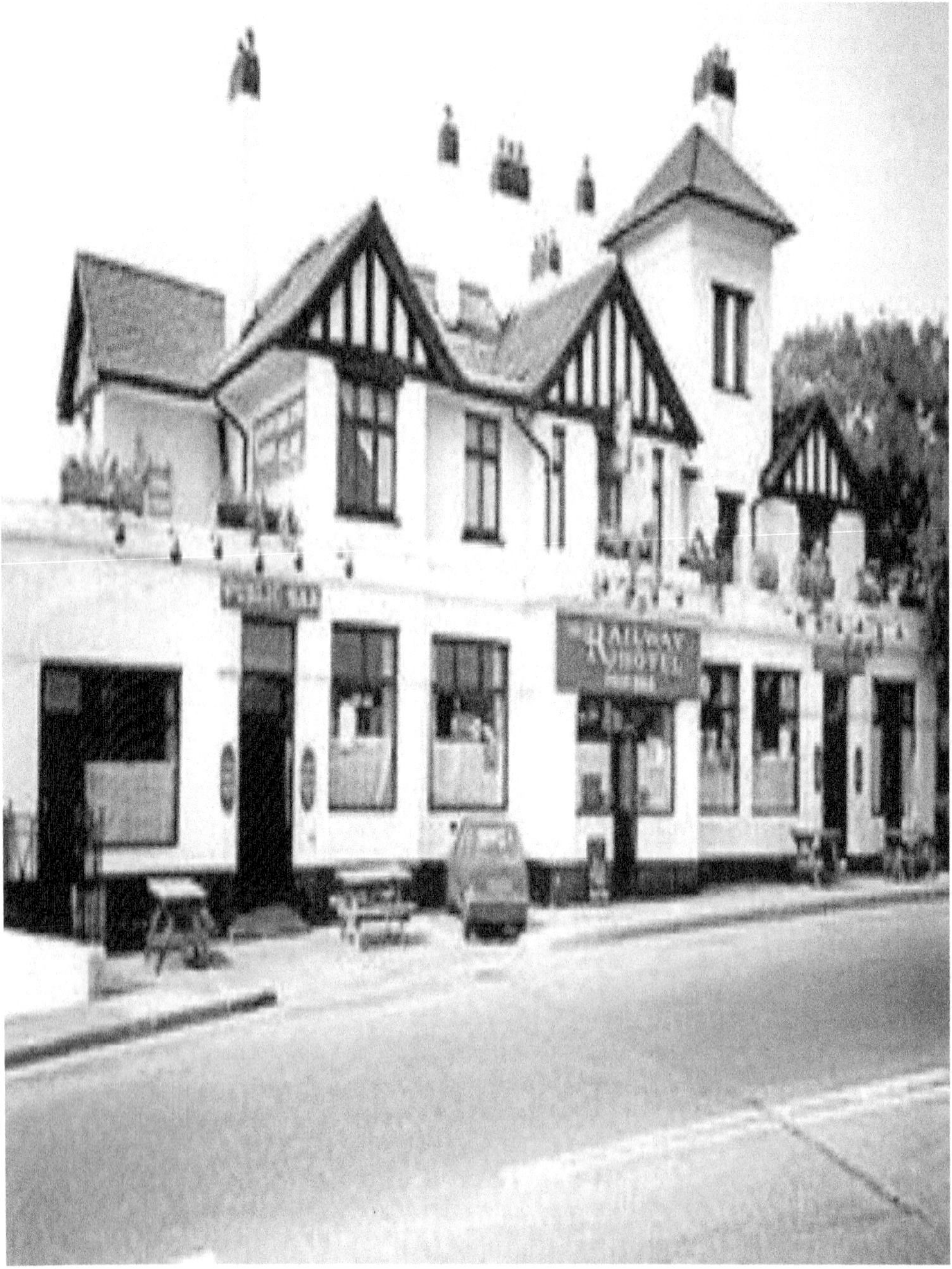

Printed in Great Britain
by Amazon